THE
POWER OF
POSITIVE
PRAYER

VOLUME 2: A-H

- 2,100 Prayer Points
- Reasons For Praying
- 8 Results of Praying

MATTHEW ASHIMOLOWO

MATTYSON MEDIA

Mattyson Media Company
P. O. Box 12961
London
E15 1UR

ISBN 1-874646-18-X

CONTENTS

1. INTRODUCTION V

2. 30 REASONS FOR PRAYER 7

3. 8 RESULTS OF PRAYER 17

PRAYER TOPICS

Abundance 21
Accomplishment 27
Affection 31
Anointing 35
Anxiety 41
Attainment 47
Attitude 53
Barrenness 57
Blessing 63
Breaking the Curse 73
Change 81
Cheerfulness 85
Comfort 89
Commitment 95
Compassion 99
Concentration 109
Confidence 113
Consecration 117
Courage 121
Decision 127
Deliverance 129
Difficult People 135
Diligence 141

Divine Acceleration 147
Divine Elevation 153
Divine Favour 159
Divine Vindication 167
Dominion 175
Encouragement 181
Endurance 187
Example 191
Faith... 195
Faithfulness of God 199
Family 203
Fear 209
Finance 213
Focus 221
Forgiveness 225
Freedom from Bondage 229
Fruitfulness 237
Future 243
Glory.. 249
Growth 253
Guidance 259
Healing 267
Honour 275
Hunger for Righteousness 279

WHO I AM IN CHRIST **285**

INTRODUCTION

The injunction *'men ought to pray and not faint'* is more applicable today with the world becoming more and more like a *'pressure cooker'*.

A person's attitude to prayer improves as he knows what prayer is all about, why he should pray and what happens when he prays.

So, let us first examine what Prayer is:

⇨   Prayer is the Christian's pilgrim staff to walk with God always.

⇨   It is a mine that is full of rich supernatural minerals to be brought out.

⇨   Prayer is heaven unruffled by storm.

⇨   When we engage in prayer, we realise the fact that it is the root, the fountain and the mother of a thousand blessings.

That is why the song writer aptly captured it:

> **Oh what peace we often forfeit**
> **Oh what needless pain we bear**
> **All because we do not carry**
> **Everything to God in prayer**

James describes prayer, particularly that of a

righteous man, as that which *'makes tremendous power available'*. He said such prayer is dynamic in its working.

Furthermore,

⇨ Prayer really is verbalising what we see in our spirit.

⇨ It is an expression of a desired expectation.

⇨ We are told that the expectation of the righteous will be fulfilled.

Attitude To Prayer:

"Sadly, in some places where prayer meetings are organised, attendance is low and the reason is revealing. When people are asked, there is seems to be a global similarity in their response, *'it is only a prayer meeting'*. They fail to realise that prayer is the capital of the believer, as money is the capital for business".

30 REASONS FOR PRAYER

The body that is not sustained with food can only stay alive for a number of days. So is the spirit of man without prayer. It becomes dead, dormant, or latent.

1.   **The Lord Jesus Christ Himself is the supreme argument for prayer.**

We are told in scriptures that He prayed:

[a]   At the grave of a dead man;
[b]   At the gate of a lost city;
[c]   In the garden of Gethsemane;
[d]   He prayed in the morning;
[e]   He took time away from His disciples to pray;
[f]   He prayed all night

"And being in anguish, he prayed more earnestly and his sweat was like drops of blood falling to the ground." [Luke 22:44]

2. **God anticipated human problems arising and made provision for a line of communication** to exist between Him and humanity.

> *"Let us then fearlessly and confidently and boldly draw near to the throne of grace [the throne of God's unmerited favour to us sinners], that we may receive mercy [for our failures] and find grace to help in good time for every need [appropriate help and well-timed help, coming just when we need it]."*
> *[Hebrews 4:16 Amp]*

3. **The true test of any genuine Christian work is revealed by the prevalence of prayer.**

> *"Now in the church [assembly] at Antioch there were prophets [inspired interpreters of the will and purposes of God] and teachers: Barnabas, Simeon who was called Niger [Black], Lucius of Cyrene, Manaen a member of the court of Herod the tetrarch, and Saul. While they were worshipping the Lord and fasting, the Holy Spirit said, Separate now for Me Barnabas and Saul for the work to which I have called them." [Acts 13:12 Amp]*

4. There is need for prayer in the church, because **there is so much of the physical and less of the spiritual.**

The twentieth century church is now strong in organising and weak on agonising. There is a lot of singing and very little of clinging to God. The church's need today is to discover the closet of prayer again.

5.   **We have a mandate to pray.**

*"And he spake a parable unto them to this end,
that men ought always to pray, and not to faint."
[Luke 18:1]*

6.   **The church must pray; that is where its
strength lies.**

7.   The church must pray, because **that is one of
the things that distinguishes her from ordinary
social gatherings in the world.**

We fail to realise that prayer is the capital of
the believer, as money is the capital for business.

8.   **We are under attack** corporately as a church
and separately as individuals. The enemy is waging
a final war against the church of Jesus Christ. This
means that if the church would take its proper place,
it ought to dictate the destiny of nations.

Satan's intention is to paralyse your plan, abort
your dreams, dilute your hope, distract your mind
and overwhelm you with a sense of hopelessness.

9.   **Prayer creates hunger for souls.**

This hunger leads to prayer. It is important to
pray in order for us to have a true vision of the lost
condition of mankind without Christ.

*"When he saw the crowds, he had compassion
on them, because they were harassed and*

helpless, like sheep without a shepherd. Then
he said to his disciples, The harvest is plentiful
but the workers are few, ask the Lord of the
harvest, therefore, to send out workers into his
harvest field". [Matthew 9:36-38]

10. The praying soul gets understanding:

The desire to know the future is engraved in
human hearts.

Paul said :

"[For I always pray to] the God of our Lord
Jesus Christ, the Father of glory, that He may
grant you a spirit of wisdom and revelation [of
insight into mysteries and secrets] in the [deep
and intimate] knowledge of Him.

By having the eyes of your heart flooded with
light, so that you can know and understand the
hope to which He has called you, and how rich
is His glorious inheritance in the saints [His set-
apart ones]." [Ephesians 1:17-18 Amp]

11. The eleventh reason for warring against the devil is because he has already declared war against mankind by his rebellion against our Maker, by

deception of the first Adam, and his attack on the last
Adam, the Lord Jesus Christ.

12. To establish the rulership of Jesus and expand the kingdom of our Lord Jesus, the last Adam who

came to take the rulership after man lost his right to
satan. Spiritual warfare is one certain way of reclaiming
the ground hitherto occupied by the enemy.

13. **To push back satanic encroachment on the church.** The closer we are to the final deliverance of the church from the earth, the fiercer the battle becomes.

> *"And I heard a voice in the midst of the four beasts say, A measure of wheat for a penny and three measures of barley for a penny; and see thou hurt not the oil and the wine."*
> *[Revelation 6:6]*

14. **To discover and deal with the stronghold of the enemy.** If there are strong men then there will be strongholds.

15. **Furthermore we need to dispossess the enemy.**

> *"Or else how can one enter into a strong man's house, and spoil his goods, except he first bind the strong man and then he will spoil his house."*
> *[Matthew 12:29]*

John reveals to us in John 10:10

> *"The thief cometh not, but for to steal, and to kill and to destroy: I am come that they might have life and that they might have it more abundantly."*

16. **To break satanic curses:**

> *"Christ hath redeemed us from the curse of the law, being made a curse for us: for it is written, Cursed is every one that hangeth on a tree."*
> *[Galatians 3:13]*

The book of Deuteronomy chapter 28 shows that poverty, sickness and barrenness are curses of the law. Why is it that believers find themselves, after salvation, with a good profession , good salary and happy family, still experiencing a deep sense of a lack of fulfilment? Why is it that it seems like one is always chasing after shadows and never really seems to arrive? Could curses inherited from parents, grandparent, the family in general still militate against the believer? Just as we had to appropriate the provision of salvation into our lives in order to be saved and just as it is necessary to appropriate the provision of healing before we can be healed, so we need to appropriate the provision of deliverance from curses in order to break the unseen boundaries built around us to contain us.

17.   **We need to deliver the city we live in from the control of satan.**

> *"For we wrestle not against flesh and blood, but against principalities, against powers, against the rulers of the darkness of this world, against spiritual wickedness in high places."*
> *[Ephesians 6:12]*

18.   Another important reason is that **warfare prayer helps us as we engage in battle** because thereby we keep the church clear and on fire.

> *"He that hath an ear, let him hear what the Spirit saith unto the Churches: To him that overcometh will I give eat of the hidden manna and will give*

*him a white stone and in the stone a new name
written, which no man knoweth saving he that
receiveth it."   [Revelation 2:17]*

19.   **Prayer helps us to deliver the nations.**

Scripture says the whole world lies under the
influence of the evil one. The empire of Persia was
under the control of a mighty demonic prince, until
Michael the archangel, was sent to help Daniel in
his spiritual battle.

> *"But the prince of the kingdom of Persia
> withstood me one and twenty days: but, lo,
> Michael, one of the chief princes, came to help
> me; and I remained there with the kings of
> Persia."   [Daniel 10:13]*

> *" Then said he, knowest thou wherefore I come
> unto thee? And now will I return to fight with
> the prince of Persia: and when I am gone forth,
> lo, the prince of Grecia shall come."
> [Daniel 10:20]*

20.   **There is a territorial prince over every
county, municipality, local government and
housing estate.**

21.   **Spiritual warfare is the way to the release of
breakthroughs.**

> *"And when he was come into the house, his
> disciples asked him privately, why could not we
> cast him out? And he said unto them, this kind
> can come forth by nothing, but by prayer and
> fasting."   [Mark 9:28-29]*

22.   **To raise an army for the end times.**

> *"And it shall come to pass afterward, that I will pour out my spirit upon all flesh; and your sons and your daughters shall prophesy, your old men shall dream dreams, your young men shall see visions: And also upon the servants and upon the handmaids in those days will I pour out my spirit."* *[Joel 2:28 - 29]*

23.   **To stop satanic oppression of the believers.**

> *"How God anointed Jesus of Nazareth with the Holy Ghost and with power; who went about doing good and healing all that were oppressed of the devil; for God was with him."* *[Acts 10:38]*

24.   **By our salvation we have moved out of the kingdom of satan.** This makes us targets of his oppression.

25.   **In the last days there will be a release of the Spirit of grace.**

> *"And I will pour upon the house of David and upon the inhabitants of Jerusalem, the spirit of grace and supplications: and they shall look upon me whom they have pierced and they shall mourn for him, as one mourneth for his only son and shall be in bitterness for him as one that is in bitterness for his first-born."* *[Zechariah 12:10]*

26.   **To protect our lives and that of our family.**

Satan does not play fair; he does not believe in

fighting you with fairness. He attacks our family with ferocity, unleashing the spirit of strife, tension and rebellion against us.

27. To shake the house of God before it is shaken.

> *"Sanctify ye a fast, call a solemn assembly, gather the elders and all the inhabitants of the land into the house of the Lord your God and cry unto the Lord." [Joel 1: 14]*

28. To break free from satanic control. Satan is a controlling spirit; he will use various kinds of dependants, such as drugs and alcohol.

> *"He that committeth sin is of the devil; for the devil sinneth from the beginning. For this purpose he Son of God was manifested that he might destroy the works of the devil." [1 John 3:8]*

> *"The Spirit of the Lord God is upon me; because the Lord hath anointed me to preach good tidings unto the meek; he hath sent me to bind up the brokenhearted, to proclaim liberty to the captive and the opening of the prison to them that are bound." [Isaiah 61:1]*

29. To usher in the revival which will precede the coming of the Lord.

> *"That which the locust ate, that which the cankerworm and the palmerworm destroyed." [Joel 2:23]*

30.   This war **is to sharpen the edge of the church and prepare her for heaven.** Heaven is for overcomers; it has pleased God to leave satan and his host as opposition for our spiritual exercise.

8 RESULTS FOR PRAYER

In the words of James, prayer produces and makes tremendous power available.

1.   When we pray we discover that it brings **personal brokenness.** Our sense of hopelessness without God becomes apparent during the time of waiting in prayer.

2.   **Spiritual sensitivity:** when Daniel completed twenty-one days of waiting on God, his ears and eyes were opened to receive. The line of communication became very clear. He was able to hear from God.

Do you still wonder about what would happen if you pray?

3.   **Hell loses its grip on souls**. That is why Jesus said we should pray to the Lord of the harvest. The power of the evil one is broken and men find it easy

to come to God in an atmosphere saturated by prayer.

4.   **Prayer pushes back darkness.** Dr. Paul Yonggi Cho, the Pastor of Full Gospel Central Church in Seoul, Korea, the world's largest church with 900,000 members, is known for saying that any believer can come to their church, preach the gospel in his pulpit and thousands will come forward to give their lives to Christ, because the church has saturated the place with prayer and thus has pushed back the hand of darkness from the location where it is.

5.   **Possess the future.**

"For I know the plans I have for you, declares the Lord, plans to prosper you and not to harm you, plans to give you hope and a future."
[Jeremiah 29:11]

Many will reach eternity and discover their wasted destiny. Like Israel, they did not enter and possess their inheritance by faith.

Through prayer we can possess ahead, days and years to come. As a matter of fact when you are waiting on God in prayer and fasting, it is not particularly for the need that has just arisen, but serves as a deposit for the blessings ahead. In the past, I had the misconception that whenever I am holding a crusade, I should be praying and teaching at the same time. I found I lacked the strength to effectively communicate the word of God, or pray for the sick. I came to understand that through prayer, tremendous results and power can be made available and it does not have to be at the time the need arose.

6.   Similar to the previous points, we **increase our arsenal for the day of our adversity**. The Bible says:

> *"If thou faint in the day of adversity, thy strength is small."* *[Proverbs 24:10]*

This passage seems to convey the idea that you must have obtained the strength, before the day in question. No army goes to war and wins by manufacturing its armour on the battle ground.

7.   **Possessing the gates of the enemy.**   Whether it is aware of this fact or not, the church holds the balance of power in the world of politics, as well as the spiritual destiny of a nation or nations. The praying church could decide the course of human events in any location.

8.   **Experience God's ability to supply.**

With all these results, you cannot but desire to pray especially when you look into the Bible and remember that:

⇨   When Daniel prayed, the mouths of the lions

were shut.

⇨   When Hannah prayed, her barren womb was opened.

⇨   When the church prayed, iron gates opened for Peter.

⇨   When Jesus prayed, Lazarus rose from the dead.

What do you think will happen when you pray?

A church may run without prayer, but it will not take long before it discovers that it cannot produce or sustain spiritual results through a carnal means.

ABUNDANCE

Genesis 15:1	Genesis 16:10	Genesis 17:6
Genesis 30:43	Exodus 1:7	Numbers 14:7
1 Kings 10:23	1 Kings 10:7	Jeremiah 31:14
2 Samuel 12:2	1 Chronicles 22:5	2 Chronicles 9:6
2 Chronicles 32:27	Psalm 21:6	Ezekiel 37:10
2 Corinthians 4:17	Ephesians 1:19	Ephesians 3:20

1. Pray that according to the promise of the Lord, your soul will be satisfied with abundance.
2. Pray that your heaven, which is like brass will soften and give rain.
3. Sever every control of the spirit of poverty over your life in the name of the Lord.
4. Praise the name of the Lord for His arm of blessing and favour.
5. Thank God for giving you His kind of life in abundance in the name of Jesus.
6. Pray that the Lord will do exceedingly great things in your life.
7. Pray for the breakthrough of abundance

beyond your imagination in Jesus name.

8. Pray for the joy of the Lord to abound in your life in the name of Jesus.

9. Receive breakthrough in the area of your business in the name of Jesus.

10. Pray for a breaking forth of God's favour in your life.

11. Pray that the grace of God will abound for you in all areas of life.

12. Thank the Lord because He will make you to know the abundance of His mercy in your life.

13. Pray that the abundant treasure of God will open unto you in the name of Jesus.

14. Give God praise for His long-suffering and goodness that is abundant towards us.

15. Pray that the abundance of God, which comes with peace and not trouble, will flow into your life.

16. Pray that the abundance of breakthrough coming your way will come with honour.

17. Ask the Lord to anoint your eyes to see the hidden riches of this world.

18. Ask the Lord to make you an example of His breakthrough in the land.

19. Receive grace to worship the Lord with that which He is bringing into your life.

20. Command that every hidden treasure of abundance be exposed to you.

21. Pray that the riches of the ungodly will enter into your hand for favour and blessing.

What?
I command? wild

22. Command God's multiplication on all that belongs to you, that it will grow exceedingly.

23. Pray for the anointing of creativity in your life and business.

24. Ask the Lord to anoint your ear to hear what God has in store for you.

25. Pray for an outbreak of the rain of God's favour in your life.

26. Pronounce on yourself that you will rise above the unbelievers around you.

27. Pray that the abundance in your life will exceed what people have heard.

28. Pray that the Lord will be your exceeding great reward in Jesus name.

29. Pray that the Lord will make you exceedingly great and fruitful.

30. Ask the Lord to make your spiritual land good and fruitful.

31. Thank the Lord for bringing your way things that are good and God glorifying.

32. Command God's prosperity on your business and ventures in the name of Jesus.

33. Receive increase in the area of wisdom, knowledge, and divine creativity in the name of Jesus.

34. Pray that the Lord will make you to become a reference point of His blessing.

35. Command the life of God into every project you have, that seems to have died.

36. Pray for an invasion of the joy that is

exceeding in your life.

37. Give praise to God for His promise to do that which exceeds your prayer, thought and dream.

38. Pray that the breakthroughs, which will follow your life, will always exceed expectations.

39. Pray that the power of God will abound in its demonstration in your life.

40. Thank the Lord for the joy that is increasing for you even in the midst of your tribulation.

41. Ask the Lord to bring forth His glory out of the challenges you are facing.

42. Pray that the tribulation will produce an eternal weight of glory.

43. Receive the blessing of God, which will extend to the children He has given to you.

44. Pray that the Lord will uphold you, not to be moved by the prosperity of the wicked.

45. Pray that the place of your dwelling will show the goodness of the Lord.

46. Command that every drought and famine area in your life will be transformed to abundance.

47. Command that the abundance of the land and sea be turned to you in Jesus name.

48. Pray that you will abound with godly contentment in all you do.

49. Give God praise for the blessing of Zion that is already flowing your way.

50. Ask the Lord to bless you with the abundance that will make you a promoter of His

kingdom.

51. Thank the Lord for causing the grace of sufficiency to abound to you.

52. Confess that according to the word of God you shall eat your bread to the full.

53. Pray that the covenant of God's blessing will be manifest in your life.

54. Thank the Lord for His promise to look favourably at your life and bless you.

CONFESSION

I believe and confess that God's abundance flows into my life. The Lord will do exceedingly great things in my life, for the breakthrough of abundance beyond my imagination rests upon my life. I shall experience blessing in every area of my business and home. The grace of God abounds unto me, the Lord opens unto me His abundant treasure. The Lord causes long-suffering and goodness that is abundant towards me to increase.

I boldly command every hidden treasure of abundance to be exposed to me that the riches of the ungodly will enter into my hand for favour and blessing, and I shall know the grace of God without trouble. I believe and confess that the Lord anoints my eyes to see the hidden riches of this world. He causes creativity to flow in my life and business, my ears are anointed to hear what God is saying, my eyes are anointed to see what God has in store, my hands are anointed to touch the blessings set aside for me. There shall be an outbreak of the rain of God's favour in my life. For the Lord will cause my life to be exceedingly blessed. The Lord will cause me to enter His great favour.

I boldly confess that God makes my spiritual life good and fruitful. He causes prosperity on my business and ventures. I receive by faith, wisdom, knowledge, and divine creativity to excel in life. I boldly declare that I become a point of reference to the glory of God for the Lord causes me to increase even in the midst of my tribulation and my tribulation will produce an eternal way to glory.

I boldly declare that the Lord will command every drought and famine area in my life to be transformed to abundance. He will cause His contentment to be upon me. The blessings of Zion flow into my life. The grace of sufficiency abounds unto me.

I am blessed and highly favoured.

ACCOMPLISHMENT

Leviticus 22:21
2 Chronicles 24:14
1 Kings 6:14
Jeremiah 44:25
Zechariah 4:9
Luke 18:31
John 19:30
Romans 9:28
Colossians 3:17
Hebrews 4:3
Revelations 10:7

Daniel 1:8
1 Kings 5:9
Psalm 64:6
Ezra 6:14
Matthew 7:17
Luke 22:37
Acts 20:24
2 Corinthians 8:6
Colossians 3:23
James 1:15
Revelations 11:7

1 Chronicles 28:20
1 Kings 6:9
Proverbs 13:19
Nehemiah 6:15
Luke 14:29-30
John 4:34
Acts 21:5
Galatians 6:9
2 Timothy 4:7
1 Peter 5:9

55. Pray that the Lord will make your life peculiar for Him in the midst of a thousand others.

56. Prophesy that there will be an accelerated achievement on the project you are pursuing.

57. Prophesy that there will be an accelerated achievement on the destiny of your children.

58. Prophesy that you will achieve things beyond your dream and hope, according to His power in you.

59. Thank the Lord for the grace to be committed

to your purpose.

60. Pray that your motivation in life will always be the achieving of the glory of God.

61. Pray that you will achieve the goal God has for you at this time.

62. Confess that you will make it to the prize of the high calling of God for your life.

63. Thank the Lord who gives you the courage to win in all situations.

64. Ask the Lord to help you accomplish everything you start in life.

65. Pray that the result of your labour will be fruitfulness.

66. Ask the Lord to crown your effort with good success.

67. Reject and refuse every trace of discouragement in the name of the Lord.

68. Thank God because you will reap the reward of your labour.

69. Pray that the projects you initiate will be accomplished.

70. Thank the Lord because you will not just finish, but you will finish well.

71. Ask the Lord for the grace to be a blessing to the body of Christ.

72. Reject the tendency to start well and not finish, in the name of the Lord.

73. Ask the Lord to open your eyes to avoid time wasting projects in the name of the Lord.

74. Thank the Lord because He will help you to

posses that which is your vision.

75. Take authority over the spirit of fear, and the spirit of failure.

76. Confess by faith that the Lord has set the land before you and you will possess it in the name of the Lord.

77. Pray that the word of God will achieve its purpose for which it was sent out.

78. Pray that God will bring the desires of your heart to pass in Jesus name.

79. Pray for the grace to carry out your vision in life.

80. Pray that you will be able to fulfil the vows you have made to the Lord.

81. Pray that you will be able to keep the vows you have made with your spouse in the name of Jesus.

82. Ask the Lord to help you to accomplish the projects you initiate in the name of Jesus.

83. Pray that the challenges you are going through will accomplish the purposes of God.

84. Pray that what the Lord has started in your life will not be frustrated by any circumstance you are facing.

85. Thank the Lord in advance for the joy of accomplishing your goal.

86. Praise the name of the Lord for accomplishing His purpose for your life.

87. Pray for the outstretching of God's hand to finish what He started in your life.

88. Pray for the presence of God in all that you

lay your hands to do.

89. Pray that you will finish the work of ministry, which you have laid your hands on.

90. Pray that you will finish the things for which you have laid a foundation.

91. Ask the Lord to help you so that you do not start and fail to finish.

92. Pray that God will accomplish the good work He started in you in the name of Jesus.

93. Ask for the grace to make the purposes of God your ultimate ambition.

94. Thank the Lord in advance for helping you finish your race with joy.

CONFESSION

I believe and confess that the Lord is good. His faithfulness is to all generations. He causes me to be fruitful in all my labour and crowns me with good success.

I believe and confess that everything I start will also finish well. God's grace abounds on to me as I carry out His vision for my life. The projects I initiate will be accomplished.

He who started a good thing in me, will be faithful to complete it.

I am blessed and highly favoured.

AFFECTION

1 Chronicles 29:3   John 13:34   Romans 12:8
Romans 12:10   1 Corinthians 7:32   2 Corinthians 7:15
1 Thessalonians 2:8-9   Colossians 3:2

95. Break the curse, which comes from not being compassionate to the poor.
96. Receive the grace to lead and guide others with diligence.
97. Pray that the love, which flows from your life, will be that which delights others.
98. Receive the grace to be able to love your neighbours as yourself.
99. Thank God for the grace to continue in His love.
100. Repent and break the hold of hypocritical love from controlling your life.
101. Ask the Holy Spirit to teach you how to provoke others to love and not to hatred.
102. Pray that the Lord will keep you in His love always.
103. Pray that you will be ministered to through the

love of the brethren in your challenging times.

104. Pray that the Lord will open your eyes to see those who need the ministry of comfort around you.

105. Ask the Lord to give you strength to overcome the fear of missing the right marriage partner.

106. Thank the Lord for the grace to love as Jesus did.

107. Pray for the ability to flow in unconditional love.

108. Pray for the grace to draw from the love of God at all times.

109. Ask the Lord to help you be an example of the love that flows among His people.

110. Release yourself from the stronghold of hatred in Jesus name.

111. Reject every trace of hypocrisy that may be found in you.

112. Repent of every unforgiveness and ask the Lord to cleanse you from every trace of evil in the name of the Lord.

113. Pray that you will be filled with the God-kind of affection in the name of Jesus.

114. Pray that you will receive grace to put your heart on heavenly things.

115. Thank the Lord for the heart that desires to be in the presence of God.

116. Pray for a heart of genuine compassion toward the unsaved friends you have.

117. Pray for a heart of genuine affection for people of other races in the name of Jesus.

118. Ask the Lord to give you a heart that pursues relationships to the glory of God.
119. Ask the Lord to burden your heart to build others for God.
120. Ask the Lord to give you the grace to prefer others to yourself.
121. Ask the Lord to give you genuine affection for the members of the household of faith.
122. Pray that the hurts of the past will not hinder the flow of your joy in the future.

CONFESSION

I believe and confess that the grace of God abounds unto me. God has deposited in me His unconditional love. The blood of Jesus has drawn me closer to the throne of grace.

The love of God flows from me to other people at all times. I am free from hatred. There is no trace of hypocrisy in me. The God-kind of affection operates in me and through me. My life, ministry and relationships are motivated by genuine affection. I refuse to allow the hurts of the past to stop the love of God from flowing through me.

I am blessed and highly favoured.

ANOINTING

Exodus 30:29   1 Samuel 10:6-7   1 Samuel 10:9-10
Psalm 45:7   Psalm 89:20-21   Psalm 92:10-11
Ecclesiastes 8:4   Isaiah 10:27   Isaiah 45:1
Isaiah 61:1   Isaiah 61:3   Nahum 2:1
Acts 7:55   Acts 10:38   Hebrews 3:12
Hebrews 3:19   Hebrews 1:9   1 John 2:27
1 John 3:8

123. Pray for the anointing to face the battle confronting you in the name of Jesus.
124. Receive the anointing to turn back the onslaught of the enemy in the name of Jesus.
125. Pray that your strength and anointing will be accompanied by the knowledge of the Lord.
126. Receive God's divine approval upon your ministry in the name of Jesus.
127. Pray that like Daniel you will manifest the anointing of excellence.
128. Pray for your church that it will experience a new move of the Holy Spirit.
129. Pray that revival will result in a baptism of

fire.

130. Thank the Lord for anointing and clothing His Word that comes from you with power.

131. Ask the Lord for an increase of His anointing for the challenges ahead.

132. Receive God's anointing for all your weak moments in the name of Jesus.

133. Pray that you will flow and maximise the gift of God in you.

134. Receive the anointing to pursue and achieve the calling of God for your life.

135. Thank the Lord for His divine enablement.

136. Give God the praise because the Greater One is in you.

137. Pray that the Lord will use you to destroy yokes in people's life.

138. Receive the anointing that removes burdens and destroys yokes.

139. Ask the Lord to release His holy fire that is able to purify your life in Jesus name.

140. Receive the grace for continuous fellowship with the Holy Spirit.

141. Ask the Lord for the anointing that brings joy.

142. Pray that you will be anointed to see a new vision.

143. Pray against anything that will cause you to lose the anointing in your life.

144. Ask the Lord for a truly broken and contrite heart which He can fill with His presence.

145. Pray for fresh, thick and rich oil of the

anointing of the Holy Spirit.

146. Pray for the anointing of holy joy upon your life.

147. Ask the Lord to baptise you with the anointing that will rise to any occasion in your life.

148. Pray for a heart that is totally yielded to the will of God.

149. Pray for a thirst and hunger for the deeper things of God in the name of Jesus.

150. Receive the anointing that opens up the word of God in the name of Jesus.

151. Pray that every yoke in your life will be destroyed by the power of God.

152. Receive the anointing to set people free in the name of Jesus.

153. Ask the Lord to use you to deliver those who are harassed by the devil.

154. Thank the Lord for anointing you with the oil of gladness above your fellows.

155. Receive the anointing to subdue the nations for God in Jesus name.

156. Pray for the power to withstand the evil gates of the enemy in the name of Jesus.

157. Receive the anointing that will make you disarm satanic kings and take authority.

158. Pray for the kind of anointing that makes a difference in ministry.

159. Receive the power for establishment in the area of your calling in Jesus name.

160. Thank God for anointing you to bring good tidings to those who are in need.

161. Pray for the boldness to set people free from all kinds of imprisonment.
162. Ask the Lord to use you to bring joy to those who lack it in the name of Jesus.
163. Receive the anointing to operate beyond human expectation.
164. Pray for the anointing that will make you a commander in the things of the spirit.
165. Pray that you will be a prophetic voice to your generation.
166. Pray for the kind of anointing that destroys the work of the devil.
167. Pray that the word of God in your mouth will always be a rhema word.
168. Rejoice for the strength which no force can overcome as a result of the anointing.
169. Confess by faith that you are a terror to the devil because of the anointing.
170. Thank God because the evil planned against you turns on the planners because of the anointing.
171. Pray for the anointing to walk in holiness and the power of God.
172. Pray for the ability of God that brings total victory in the name of Jesus.
173. Receive the boldness that will cause you to confront the most difficult situation.
174. Pray that your motives for the power of God will always be according to the will of God.
175. Confess that the Lord will use you for signs

and wonders to His glory.

176. Pray for the anointing to receive divine revelation at all times.

177. Pray that as you associate with those who you respect, their giftings will rub on you.

178. Express your craving for the power of God daily in the name of Jesus.

179. Like Moses pray that you will discover your own rod (gift) for doing wonders.

180. Pray that your passage through the furnace of affliction will turn on the anointing of God.

CONFESSION

I give God praise for His divine enablement. I thank God because His grace is sufficient for me at all times. He gives me confidence to face each moment.

I believe and confess that the anointing of the Holy Spirit, which remove bondages and destroy yokes, resides in me. Through me the joy of the Lord is released to those who lack it. I am anointed to subdue nations for God. The power of God resides in me to withstand the evil gadgets of the enemy.

By faith I confess that the anointing of God makes the difference in my ministry. Therefore, I am anointed to bring good tidings to those who are in need and set free people in emotional prisons.

I boldly confess that I am a prophetic voice to my generation. The word of the Lord in my mouth shall be anointed.

I am blessed and highly favoured.

ANXIETY

Psalm 142:4   Daniel 3:16   Jeremiah 17:8
Matthew 5:6   Matthew 6:24-25   Matthew 6:34
Matthew 6:21   Matthew 22:16   Luke 8:14
Luke 10:41   Romans 8:28   1 Corinthians 7:32
Philippians 3:12   Philippians 4:6   Philippians 4:10
Philippians 4:16   1 Peter 5:6-7

181. Take authority over every tendency to drift into worry and anxiety.

182. Thank the Lord for the joy that passes all understanding.

183. Reject and refuse every tendency of worry and fear in the name of the Lord.

184. Thank the Lord because the abundance of His grace is more than all your need.

185. Reject the tendency to worry over the things you cannot change in your power.

186. Thank the Lord because He will provide for all your need just as He does for the birds.

187. Release yourself from every form of

emotional bondage that results in anxiety.

188. Ask for the grace to seek after the will of God and not after things in the name of Jesus.

189. Confess that you will not bring forth for trouble or gather your possession for the day of adversity.

190. Pray that instead of worry your heart will be filled with faith.

191. Thank the Lord for turning your setbacks into stepping stones.

192. Pray that every situation that has troubled you mind will turn around for your good.

193. Confess that you will not be anxious, but commit your challenges to God.

194. Ask the Holy Spirit to come and take control of every situation that has troubled your mind.

195. Lift up your voice in advance of your situation being turned around by the Lord.

196. Ask the Lord to open your eyes to see what He wants you to learn in the situation you are in.

197. Take authority over every negative the enemy is using and destroy His weapon in Jesus name.

198. Reject every load of care the enemy wants to put on you and declare your freedom in Christ.

199. Pray for freedom over the works of evil doers.

200. Break yourself free from worry at seeing an ungodly person prosper.

201. Break the hold of fear and worry of evil men

that is holding your heart, in the name of Jesus.

202. Nullify the fear of any curse pronounced against you and your family in Jesus name.

203. Break yourself free from the fear of an economic downturn in the future.

204. Confess that you shall not be held in the grip of care and unnecessary worry.

205. Receive the boldness to stand for the truth without the fear of man.

206. Ask the Lord to help you to always approach situations of life with prayer.

207. Receive healing from the impact of fear and negative experiences in the name of Jesus.

208. Break yourself free from the fear and worry which causes eating disorders.

209. Pray for the strength to overcome the fear of the future.

210. Ask the Lord to give you strength to overcome the fear of missing the right marriage partner.

211. Pray that the Lord will give you true overseers who care for your soul.

212. Thank the Lord for opportunity to put all our cares and worries on Him.

213. Pray that your spiritual eyes will be open to stop what wants to choke the word of God in your life.

214. Thank the Lord for giving you abundance in the time of famine and taking away your fears.

215. Thank God because He will use every

situation for your good in Jesus name.

216. Pray that you will grow in your desire for the will of God.

217. Pray that God will burden your heart to pray for revival.

218. Ask the Lord to help you to always be zealous for the will of God.

219. Pray that you will increase in your pursuit of the will of God

220. Resist everything that wants to stop you from reaching your goal in Jesus name.

221. Pray for the wisdom to handle every bout of discouragement in the name of the Lord.

222. Counter everything that wants to draw you back into the life you lived outside Christ in Jesus name.

223. Ask the Lord to burden your heart for a life that glorifies God.

224. Pray that you will be full of zeal to pursue the vision God has given you.

225. Come against anything that belittles the vision God has given you.

226. Thank the Lord for the desire to overcome all obstacles.

227. Give God the praise because every attempt by satan to make you discouraged will be countered in the name of Jesus.

CONFESSION

I thank the Lord for His joy that passes understanding which flows through me. I have been set free from the tendency of worry and anxiety, in the name of the Lord. I am not afraid of the future, because my Father goes ahead of me.

I believe and confess that God has set me free from every form of emotional bondage and has filled me with godly confidence.

I boldly declare that I shall not bring forth for trouble, nor gather my possessions for the day of adversity. The load of care that the enemy placed on me is broken, in Jesus name.

I believe and confess that fear and worry are not my possessions. For all my worries I receive boldness and a sound mind. I am filled with the love of God. My future is as sure and bright as the promises of God.

I am blessed and highly favoured.

ATTAINMENT

Leviticus 22:21   **Job 14:6**   **Proverbs 1:5**
Jeremiah 44:25   **John 14:14**   **Acts 21:5**
Romans 9:30-31   **Philippians 3:11-12**   **Philippians 3:16**
Colossians 3:23   **1 Timothy 4:6**   **1 Peter 5:9**
3 John 2

228. Ask the Lord to help you to be motivated to achieve at all times in the name of Jesus.

229. Ask the Lord for the power to mount up and rise above every limitation.

230. Pray that the Lord will make your life peculiar for Him in the midst of a thousand others.

231. Prophesy that there will be an accelerated achievement on the project you are pursuing.

232. Prophesy that there will be an accelerated achievement on the destiny of your children.

233. Prophesy that you will achieve things beyond your dream and hope, according to His power in you.

234. Pray that your motivation in life will always

be the achieving of the glory of God.

235. Pray that you will achieve the goal God has for you at this time.

236. Confess that you will make it to the prize of the high calling of God for your life.

237. Thank the Lord because success will attend everything you do.

238. Bless God for providing everything you need for life and godliness.

239. Thank God for the power and authority in the name of Jesus.

240. Commit your needs to God and believe that He will supply in the name of Jesus.

241. Present your needs to God and believe that they will come to pass.

242. Release every blessing of yours that the enemy is hindering in Jesus name.

243. Pray that you will obtain favour in the sight of the king like Esther did in the name of Jesus.

244. Pray that grace and favour will always flow to you from the people around you.

245. Give thanks to the Lord for making joy and gladness your portion in the name of Jesus.

246. Thank the Lord because you shall come to His sanctuary to testify of His goodness.

247. Pray that no matter what you go through, you shall yet come to Zion with singing.

248. Pray that you will obtain the favour that comes with the wisdom of the Lord.

249. Ask the Lord to help you walk in the

righteousness of Christ and to obtain His favour.

250. Thank the Lord in advance for achieving success in your home in Jesus name.

251. Pray that the vision you see will become a reality in your life in the name of Jesus.

252. Receive the grace from the Lord that will make you hold on to the day of the breakthrough.

253. Receive the faith that will help you obtain the testimony of entering the promises of God.

254. Come against every selfish lust towards that which is not of God in the name of Jesus.

255. Thank the Lord in advance because your effort will not be in vain in the name of Jesus.

256. Ask for the grace to keep running until you obtain the promise in the name of Jesus.

257. Ask the Lord to help you run and finish the Christian race well in the name of Jesus.

258. Count your blessing in the Lord, see what God has done and refuse to be discouraged before adversity.

259. Receive the boldness to approach and enjoy the presence of the Lord.

260. Pray that the ministry God has given you will increase and be excellent.

261. Receive the anointing to prosper in the name of the Lord.

262. Sever every control of the spirit of poverty over your life in the name of the Lord.

263. Confess by faith that everything you lay your hands on will result in prosperity.
264. Pray that your spiritual vision will come to pass.
265. Confess by faith that divine understanding will cause you to attain wise counsel.
266. Pray that you will remain in the faith and finish the race well.
267. Pray that you will grow daily in the grace and knowledge of the Lord.
268. Thank God for His hand that has been upholding you through the challenges of life.
269. Destroy every stronghold of satan that is holding you from reaching your spiritual goal.
270. Pray that the word of God will continue to work in your life in the name of Jesus.
271. Pray that everything you experience will resulting your spiritual growth and blessing.
272. Thank God because He will uphold you to the end of your Christian walk.
273. Declare that every weapon targeted at your peace will turn around for your blessing.

CONFESSION

I believe and confess that the Lord is good. His faithfulness extends to the heavens. God is my Father and He provides all my needs through Christ Jesus.

By faith I present all challenges to Him and boldly declare that I have victory through Him.

I believe and confess that I have received the anointing to prosper. I have been broken free from the spirit and control of poverty. My blessings which the enemy has hindered have been released right now. The stronghold of satan have been destroyed right now. I will attain God's purpose and destiny for me.

I am blessed and highly favoured.

ATTITUDE

Deuteronomy 30:19   Judges 20:22   1 Samuel 30:6
Proverbs 10:4-5   Proverbs 12:11   Proverbs 12:24
Proverbs 13:11   Proverbs 19:15   Proverbs 20:13
Proverbs 22:29   Daniel 1:8   Matthew 5:16
John 14:15   Romans 12:11   Romans 12:16
Philippians 2:5   Colossians 3:22-23   1 Thessalonians 4:11-12
2 Thessalonians 3:10   2 Timothy 1:6-7

274. Thank the Lord for the grace to be committed to your purpose.

275. Thank the Lord for giving you a reason to laugh in life.

276. Pray for a godly attitude that will influence other people and glorify God.

277. Ask the Lord for a positive attitude inside that will change the outside.

278. In times of trouble, draw strength, encouragement and help from the Holy Spirit.

279. Ask the Lord to anoint your eyes to see how your problems can turn to solutions.

280. Pray that the Lord will use you as light for the

darkness in this world.

281. Ask the Lord to uproot the negatives of the past that will hinder you from entering His purpose.

282. Pray for a heart that is single-minded in serving the Lord.

283. In the time of discouragement, pray that your face will be set like a flint towards heaven.

284. Pray that you will stay within the revealed plan of God for your life.

285. Break every limitation that is trying to stop you from entering where you have never been.

286. Cancel every satanic intimidation with the blood of Jesus.

287. Ask the Lord to reveal any negative attitude that is shutting doors against you.

288. Pray for the grace of a single-minded commitment to the call of God for your life.

289. Ask the Lord to help you lead a life that glorifies God.

290. Pray that your life will be a source of light to those in the darkness of this world.

291. Ask the Lord to help you live a life that is a testimony to the glory of God.

292. Pray that your life will draw people to the gospel of Christ.

293. Thank the Lord because He will use you to challenge people to a higher life in Him.

294. Pray that the Lord will teach you to be a repairer of the breach between you and those

who have offended you.

295. Reverse every curse pronounced against you in the name of Jesus.

296. Ask the Lord to teach you how to be a source of healing to those who hate you.

297. Pray that the Lord will use every persecution you face result in your promotion in the name of the Lord.

298. Release the grace and wisdom of the Holy Spirit in every situation in the name of Jesus.

299. Pray that every action of yours will be motivated by the love of God.

300. Thank the Lord for sending men and women who share your vision and commitment in the name of the Lord.

301. Ask the Holy Spirit for the grace of humility and a heart after the will of God.

302. Release the anointing of Heaven's wisdom into your life in the name of Jesus.

303. Pray that your attitude will be influenced by the mind-set of the kingdom of God.

CONFESSION

I believe and confess that the Lord is good, He has changed my mourning into dancing. He has given me a reason to laugh in life, no matter what I go through.

I believe and confess that it will be all right, for the Lord shall be my strength and encouragement for the light and darkness of this world.

I believe and confess that no matter what I go through, and in the face of discouragement, only the purpose and counsel of God will stand. Neglect of the past will become my stepping-stone. The limitation I have known will become my source of breakthrough. Every satanic limitation is destroyed, in the name of the Lord. Every persecution I face will result in promotion.

I am blessed and highly favoured.

BARRENNESS

Genesis 11:30   Genesis 25:21   Exodus 23:26
Deuteronomy 7:13   Deuteronomy 7:14   1 Samuel 2:20
Psalm 113:9   Proverbs 30:15-16 Isaiah 54:1
Galatians 4:27

304. Pray that your wife will give birth to the children that will bring glory to God.
305. Command that every root of barrenness in your life will break forth with fruit bearing.
306. Ask the Lord to help you to move from mere fruit bearing to bearing much fruit.
307. Thank the Lord for delivering you from spiritual barrenness.
308. Pray that you will experience fruitfulness in the area where there has been barrenness in your life.
309. Pray that the promotion of the Lord in your life will move you from barrenness to fruitfulness.
310. Cancel the curse that may have caused

spiritual barrenness in the name of the Lord.

311. Cancel every bondage of genetic diseases in your family to ten generations.

312. Prophesy the blessing of children into the life of any barren person you know.

313. Receive the blessing of your man of God that will unlock your hidden blessing.

314. Pray for the barren women you know that they will become joyful mothers of children.

315. Curse every root of barrenness in the life of your loved ones.

316. Give Him praise because He will not withhold any good thing from you in the name of the Lord.

317. Come against all manifestations of barrenness in the form of retention, locked-up wombs and hindrances in the name of the Lord.

318. Declare that there shall be none barren in your home in the name of the Lord.

319. Pray that every area of your life that is yearning for supply from God will be filled in the name of the Lord.

320. Ask the Lord to stop those areas of barrenness in your life in Jesus name.

321. Thank the Lord for His promise to make you fruitful in all things.

322. Prophesy fruitfulness to every area of your ministry in the name of Jesus.

323. Confess and renounce all the sins or mistakes that may have caused your barrenness.

324. Pray that your faith will grow as Sarah's own grew in the times of her waiting.

325. As was spoken into the life of Rebecca, confess that one day your children will possess the gates of their enemies.

326. Pray that the areas that have become barren like that of Leah because you are unloved will receive life again.

327. Release every agony and burden of your heart, which like Rachel's has filled your heart.

328. Make a covenant with God like the mother of Samuel and dedicate the miracle you will receive to the Lord even before it happens.

329. Thank God because out of your barrenness shall come forth that which glorifies God.

330. Repent of your trusting in the arm of flesh and ask the Lord to take control.

331. Give God the praise for the breakthrough He has already given you in the name of Jesus.

332. Barrenness is caused by despising what God appreciates; ask the Lord to forgive you of such sin.

333. Pray that the Lord will fill you with harvest ideas in the name of the Lord.

334. Destroy the yoke of financial barrenness in your life.

335. Pray for a renewal in the area of vision and zeal, that you will regain your momentum.

336. Pray that you will conceive with the right seed, vision and ideas.

337. Reject every tendency of miscarriage of your seed or pregnancy in the name of the Lord.

338. Without a seed there is no harvest; pray that the Lord will open your heart to see what to sow.

339. Pray that the Lord will see you through to birthing.

340. Ask the Lord for the grace to keep asking until something happens.

341. Prophesy to your womb to come alive in the name of the Lord.

342. Pray that all the resources you have lost will be regained in the name of the Lord.

343. Take authority over every spirit of Peninah that is trying to mock you, and declare your victory.

344. Pray that the provocation of the enemy will work for your good.

345. Pray that you will not get stuck on one level of blessing.

346. Thank the Lord because even that which you thought is too late shall come to pass.

347. Pray that when your breakthrough comes it shall have every manifestation of a miracle child.

348. Declare by faith that every aspect of your life shall keep bearing fruit.

349. Thank the Lord because according to His word no area of your life will be barren.

350. Confess by faith that you shall be surrounded by the fruit of you confession.

351. Pray that the Lord will intervene and turn your

situation around.

352. Take authority over the area of continuous barrenness in your life and command that it turns-around for fruitfulness.

353. Thank the Lord in advance for putting His song of victory in your mouth.

354. Thank God because you shall not be unfruitful or barren.

355. Command any trace of barrenness in all of your undertakings to change in the name of Jesus.

CONFESSION

I believe and confess that the Lord is good and He is faithful to make His promise good.

I thank the Lord because He will not withhold from me any good thing. Every manifestation of barrenness is disappearing, in the name of Jesus. Barrenness has ceased in my life, in the name of Jesus. I shall be fruitful in all areas. Out of my barrenness shall come forth the miracle baby, the miracle job, the miracle of all that brings glory to the name of the Lord. My heart is released from the bondage of barrenness. Every aspect of my life shall keep bearing fruit, for the Lord will restore all my lost resources.

I boldly declare that I conceive with the right

seed, vision and ideas. I shall be surrounded by the fruit of my confession. The Lord has put a song of victory in my mouth, for I shall not be unfruitful or barren.

I am blessed and highly favoured.

BLESSING

Genesis 12:2-3	Genesis 22:17-18	Genesis 28:3
Genesis 32:26	Genesis 49:26	Exodus 23:25
Leviticus 25:21	Numbers 6:24-25	Deuteronomy 11:26
Deuteronomy 23:5	Deuteronomy 24:19	Deuteronomy 26:15
Deuteronomy 28:8	Deuteronomy 33:11	Joshua 17:14
Joshua 17:16-18	Joshua 24:13	Ruth 2:4
1 Samuel 2:20	2 Samuel 6:11	1 Kings 18:41
1 Chronicles 4:10	2 Chronicles 6:3	Psalm 1:1
Psalm 3:8	Psalm 5:12	Psalm 16:7
Psalm 29:11	Psalm 32:1	Psalm 41:1
Psalm 84:5	Psalm 89:15	Psalm 128:5
Psalm 132:15	Proverbs 8:32	Proverbs 10:6
Proverbs 10:22	Proverbs 11:11	Proverbs 11:26
Proverbs 20:7	Proverbs 28:20	Isaiah 44:3
Isaiah 65:8	Ezekiel 44:30	Daniel 2:6
Zechariah 8:13	Malachi 3:10	Ephesians 1:3
1 Peter 3:9		

356. Give the Lord praise for setting you on a roller coaster of blessing which no man can stop.

357. Pray that your eyes will be open not to miss your breakthrough in the name of Jesus.

358. Pray that the abundance of breakthrough coming your way will come with honour.

359. Ask the Lord to anoint your eyes to see the hidden riches of this world.
360. Break the cycle of poverty and confess that your soul shall be satisfied.
361. Pray that you will not just be a channel of blessing, but you will enjoy the blessing too.
362. Thank the Lord for His transfer of the wealth of the ungodly to the righteous.
363. Pray for the accelerated breakthrough of the plough man overtaking the reaper.
364. Thank the Lord for the day when the treader of grapes will overtake seed sowers.
365. Pray that the days when harvest will meet harvest will be manifest in your life.
366. Thank the Lord for loving you and lifting you out of the dust of defeat.
367. Pray that the Lord who lifts out of the dust will bring His promotion to your life.
368. Thank the Lord for loving you and lifting you out of the dust of defeat.
369. Pray that the Lord who lifts out of the dust will bring His promotion to your life.
370. Reverse the curse pronounced against your source of income.
371. Confess by faith that there is a sound of rain, even in the midst of spiritual dryness.
372. Repent of the spirit of materialism which has manifested itself in those who have withheld what they should give God.
373. Repent on behalf of your city for the sins that

may have brought a closed Heaven in Jesus name.

374. Prophecy into your future that God will begin to bring to you the riches of the Gentiles.

375. Ask the Lord to burden your heart to sow into other people's life.

376. Release every blessing of yours which the enemy is hindering in Jesus name.

377. Thank the Lord for giving you abundance in the time of famine and taking away your fears.

378. Thank the Lord for His manifold blessing to us who trust in Him.

379. Thank the Lord who always causes us to have victory in Him.

380. Pray for divine fruitfulness in all that you do.

381. Confess by faith that according to God's word He will elevate you in what you do.

382. Pray for an all-round favour and blessing which cannot be overlooked.

383. Lay hand on every project you are executing and pray that it will experience God's favour.

384. Receive a turnaround breakthrough from the Lord.

385. Break the hold of every evil pronouncement made into your life in the past in Jesus name.

386. Break every generational curse militating against your destiny.

387. Plead the blood of Jesus against every family trait that is negative.

388. Speak the blessing of the Lord on everything you have.

389. Receive the breakthrough of divine acceleration from the Lord in Jesus name.

390. Receive the blessing of God's divine protection in the name of Jesus.

391. Pray that the glory of the Lord will rest on all that you have.

392. Thank God for His marvellous grace that is abounding to you.

393. Pray that the Lord will lead you to be in the exact location of your destiny.

394. Receive the blessing of the Lord for all the works of your hand.

395. Ask the Lord to open your eyes to that which can provoke His curse on your work.

396. Prophesy on the labour of your hand that it shall manifest what God has spoken into your life.

397. Confess that the covenant of God's blessing shall come to pass.

398. Command the blessing of the Lord on all that represents your storehouse.

399. Thank the Lord in advance for putting His blessing on all that you set out to do.

400. Speak the blessing of the Lord on all your children and the future generation.

401. Confess the blessing of the Lord in advance of your expected breakthrough.

402. Come against every limitation which the enemy is trying to put on your life.

403. Pray that the Lord will network you with people who will believe in your vision.

404. Receive the blessing of your man of God that will unlock your hidden blessing.

405. Receive the blessing of the fruit of the womb in the name of Jesus.

406. Pray that the presence of the Lord will convey His blessing anywhere you are.

407. Prophesy change to every prevailing circumstance you are facing.

408. Break every barrier that is holding you from entering a new realm of blessing.

409. Receive God's divine endorsement on that which you are doing.

410. Pray for an outbreak of the blessing of God in your church.

411. Thank the Lord for surrounding and shielding you with His favour.

412. Thank the Lord for the favour of His leading and direction in your life.

413. Speak the peace of God to every situation that has troubled your mind.

414. Receive the blessing that flows from His throne to His own in the name of Jesus.

415. Pray for God's divine provision for the fulfilment of your life's vision.

416. Cancel every ungodly counsel that will draw you from God's plan.

417. Confess that your confidence in the Lord shall not be put to shame.

418. Thank the Lord for the blessing of His forgiveness and cleansing from sin.

419. Pray that the Lord will use your blessing to touch those who are less privileged.

420. Thank the Lord for His grace that sought you out and favoured you with His blessing.

421. Rejoice in the fact that your confidence and strength is in the Lord.

422. Pray that the sound of joy and thanksgiving will not cease in your house.

423. Ask the Lord for the blessed heart that remains humble.

424. Pray that you will grow in the grace to accept the chastisement of the Lord.

425. Pray that no matter what breakthrough you have it will not draw you into a life of sin.

426. Pray that the entrance of God's word will always produce transformation in your life.

427. Ask the Lord to anoint your ears to hear Him at all times.

428. Pray that you will reap a bumper harvest from every seed you have sown.

429. Prophesy into the future of your children that they will manifest God's blessing.

430. Receive the grace to wait for God's time of favour for your life.

431. Prophesy the blessing of children into the life of any barren person you know.

432. Ask the Lord to make you a giver in His kingdom.

433. Pray that your children will be a blessing and not a curse to their generation.
434. Pray that God will use what you have to bless the nations in Jesus name.
435. Pray that God will give you the kind of favour that will make your children rise and call you blessed.
436. Confess that according to the word of God you shall be a blessing.
437. Stand against anything that will steal the blessing designated for your life.
438. Thank the Lord because you shall never leave His presence empty handed.
439. Like Joseph, pray that the blessing of the Lord will always follow you.
440. Receive the blessing of the Lord on all that you have both at home and abroad.
441. Thank the Lord by faith for the favour of operating under an open heaven.
442. Release every hidden blessing belonging to you in Jesus name.
443. Thank the Lord for the children He is bringing into your life, whether biological or spiritual.
444. Prophesy that the blessing of the Lord shall prevail no matter what.
445. Give the Lord praise because He will help you to possess your possession.
446. Consecrate yourself in preparation for a new level of blessing.
447. Ask the Lord to command His blessing and

favour upon your coming years.

448. Confess that you choose to walk in the blessing of the Lord and reject every curse.

449. Receive the blessing which follows the walk of obedience in the name of Jesus.

450. Command that every curse pronounced against you will turn to blessing.

451. Nullify the effect of any curse against your future in the name of Jesus.

452. Command that all the blessings of the Lord come on you and your family.

453. Command that any evil pronouncement of those who are envious will turn to your blessing.

454. Thank the Lord for putting His blessing upon His people in the name of Jesus.

455. Pray that your destiny will become manifest for all to see.

456. Reject every trace of sorrow as the Lord increases you in Jesus name.

457. Pray for the blessing that leads to God's kind of riches in the name of the Lord.

458. Pray that the breakthrough in your life will bless your city.

459. Ask the Lord to make you a blessing to your generation.

460. Ask the Lord to help you in using your gifts to bless other people.

461. Thank the Lord because of His promise that you will abound in blessing.

462. Receive the promise of God's blessing on

your offspring.

463. Pray that the Lord will bring forth His beauty out of your setback.

464. Pray that you will enter the realm of God's blessing that is a shower.

465. Pray that you will receive the priestly blessing of your pastor.

466. Pray that just as in your past you have hurt people, in your future you will be a blessing.

467. Thank the Lord for the out poured blessing which follows obedience in tithing.

468. Rejoice because God has blessed you with all spiritual blessing in the heavenly places.

469. Pray that you will be strengthened of the Lord not to reward evil for evil.

470. Thank the Lord for the promise of His inheritance in your life in the name of Jesus.

CONFESSION

I believe and confess that the Lord is good. His manifold blessings are made known to those who trust Him. God always causes me to have victory through the Lord Jesus, as I rely on His Word. The Lord will favour me with an all round blessing which cannot be overlooked.

Every evil pronouncement militating against my life is cancelled with the blood. I break the generation curse that is militating against my understanding. I come against every limitation which the enemy is trying to put on my life.

I boldly confess the blessing of a home and financial blessing, in Jesus Name. I receive God's divine endorsement and proclaim God's divine endorsement now, in all that I do. For the Lord will favour me with His divine direction. All my hidden blessings are being exposed by the Lord. The manifestation of God's blessing shall erase the days of sorrow.

I am blessed and highly favoured.

BREAKING THE CURSE

Genesis 8:21   Genesis 12:3   Genesis 27:12
Genesis 27:29   Exodus 21:17   Exodus 22:28
Leviticus 19:14   Numbers 22:6   Numbers 23:8
Deuteronomy 11:26   Deuteronomy 24:19   Deuteronomy 27:16-26
Judges 9:27   Judges 9:57   2 Samuel 19:21
Nehemiah 13:2   Psalm 62:4   Psalm 119:21
Proverbs 11:26   Proverbs 24:24   Proverbs 28:27
Jeremiah 17:5   Jeremiah 48:10   Zechariah 8:13
Malachi 2:2   Matthew 5:44   Acts 23:12

471. Come against the spirit of spiritual slumber in the name of Jesus.

472. Break the cycle of poverty and lack that has been in your family from generations.

473. Reverse the curse of dissatisfaction in all the things you do in the name of Jesus.

474. Command that evil pronouncements of those who are envious will turn to your blessing.

475. Ask the Lord to open your eyes to that which can provoke His curse on your work.

476. Ask the Lord to deliver you from the emotional baggage you inherited from your parents.

477. Break the curse of worshipping any ungodly image in your family.
478. Break the curse of disrespect for your family militating against your family.
479. Break the curse of offence committed against your neighbour dating back to generations.
480. Break the curse which comes as a result of misleading the disabled.
481. Break the curse which comes as a result of offence against a foreigner.
482. Break the impact of the curse of incest in your family in the name of Jesus.
483. Break the curse of participating in sexual sin in Jesus name.
484. Break the curse which comes as a result of bestiality.
485. Break the curse which comes with committing sin with your in-laws.
486. Break the power of the curse which comes as a result of damaging your neighbours behind their backs.
487. Break the generational curse which follows destroying the innocent without reason.
488. Break the curse which follows disobedience to the word of God.
489. Breaking the curse which may have come on your business and your income.
490. Reverse every curse pronounced against you in the name of Jesus.
491. Nullify the fear of any curse pronounced against

you and your family in Jesus name.

492. Thank the Lord for redeeming you from the curse of the law.

493. Thank the Lord for His promise to deliver those who trust in Him.

494. Break the impact of the curse of idolatry in your family to the tenth generation.

495. Break the consequence of the curse of disobedience to parent over your life.

496. Destroy the effect of every economic and financial dealing that is false in the name of Jesus.

497. Break the curse which comes from misleading the sick and the maimed.

498. Cancel the effect of the curse of taking advantage of the strangers around you.

499. Break the power of the curse of incest over your life in the name of Jesus.

500. Repent and break the hold of the curse of bestiality in your life and family.

501. Break the impact of the incestuous experience with immediate brothers or sisters in your family.

502. Break the curse of destroying the neighbours in secret in the name of Jesus.

503. Cancel the impact of receiving bribes to do injustice that may have been in your family.

504. Break the curse which follows disobedience to the Word of God.

505. Cancel every curse pronounced on your

business in the name of the Lord.

506. Break the curse pronounced over you which says you will not marry.

507. Break the curse that may have brought physical barrenness in the name of Jesus.

508. Destroy every curse that may have rested on your children.

509. Break the generational curse that may be hindering you from fulfilling your purpose.

510. Break the curse that has brought diseases in the name of Jesus.

511. Cancel the impact of the curse that makes you run from your enemies.

512. Destroy the effect of the curse that has made the heavens to be like brass.

513. Break the curse that makes you flee from the enemies seven ways.

514. Destroy the generational curse of madness and mental breakdown.

515. Cancel every generational curse that has brought economic and physical bondage.

516. Cancel the generational curse of poverty and lack back to tenth generation.

517. Break the curse of oppression and bondage from your family in the name of the Lord.

518. Break the curse of much labour and less harvest in the name of Jesus.

519. Break the bondage of servitude to those who hate you.

520. Destroy the yoke of bondage, which is a product

of curses in the name of Jesus.

521. Break the curse that makes people of your family down trodden in the name of Jesus.

522. Cancel every form of slavery, which may have ruled over your relations in the name of Jesus.

523. Cancel the curse of sowing without reaping in the name of Jesus.

524. Cancel the curse that makes people abhor you instead of favour in the name of Jesus.

525. Cancel the curse that exposes you to satanic curses in the name of the Lord.

526. Break the bondage of tendencies to go back to sins of the past.

527. Cancel every form of bondage caused by genetic diseases in your family to ten generations.

528. Cancel the curse of restlessness and the bondage of fear in your life.

529. Break the curse which shedding the blood of the innocent has brought in the name of Jesus.

530. Break the impact of the curse of sexual impurity in the name of Jesus.

531. Cancel the curse that may have caused spiritual barrenness in the name of the Lord.

532. Cancel the curse that may have alighted through disrespect for God's anointed.

533. Break the curse of dissatisfaction and emptiness in the name of the Lord.

534. Break the curse of panic and fear that grips in the name of the Lord.

535. Counter the impact of the curses that you may

have brought on yourself with the blood of Jesus.

536. Break yourself free from a curse and astonishment of heart in the name of Jesus.

537. Break the curse that comes from not being compassionate to the poor.

538. Break the curse from giving an offering that God abhors.

539. Receive the blessing that follows total obedience to the will of God.

540. Ask the Lord to forgive you and remove the consequence of deceiving people.

541. Thank the Lord in advance for turning every curse pronounced on you into a blessing.

542. Pray that the area where you may have been a curse will now much turn to a blessing.

543. Confess that you will not be a taunt, a proverb and a curse in the name of Jesus.

544. Cancel all evil pronouncements that you have made in Jesus name.

545. Counter every curse pronounced on your life by your superiors in Jesus name.

546. Counter the curse which disobedience to tithing has brought in Jesus name.

547. Break the curse which withholding from the needy may have brought in Jesus name.

548. Remove the curse which may have come through offending an anointed of God.

549. Reverse every curse that was brought by attacking your parent in Jesus name.

550. Reverse the curse that your parent may have pronounced against you.
551. Break the curse that may have come through offending and hurting the handicapped.
552. Ask the Lord to forgive those who have pronounced a curse against you unjustly.
553. Ask the Lord to forgive you for raising your hand against His anointed.
554. Reverse the curse pronounced against your source of income.
555. Reverse the curse that has come through cheating your neighbour.
556. Reverse the curse that comes through misleading the handicapped.

CONFESSION

I believe and confess that the Lord is good for He has redeemed me from the curse of the law. By faith I confess that the curse of disobedience to parents over my life is broken in the name of Jesus. Every contrary law of the enemy over me is destroyed in the name of the Lord. The effect of economic and financial dealing that is false is cancelled in the name of Jesus.

I break the curse of sickness, the curse of disease, poverty and lack that dates back to four generations in my family, in the name of Jesus. I

cancel the impact of incestuous experience. I cancel
the impact of disobedience to God, idolatry and
every form of generational curse that is hindering
me from entering the purpose of God for my life.

I believe and confess that I am free from the yoke
of bondage. I believe and confess that I am free
from the curse that makes a family down trodden.
Slavery is not my portion.

Sickness is not my portion, disease is rejected
in my life in the name of Jesus. Every hold of the
enemy is broken. Evil pronouncements made into
my life are cancelled in the name of Jesus. I thank
the Lord in advance for turning every curse into a
blessing and every challenge into His favour in
Jesus name.

CHANGE

1 Chronicles 4:10   Job 14:14   Psalm 102:26
Malachi 3:6   Matthew 18:3   1 Corinthians 15:51-52
2 Corinthians 3:18   Philippians 3:21   Hebrews 1:12
Hebrews 7:12

557. Ask the Lord to turn your transition time, to a time of transformation of life.
558. Pray that your confessions will always bring forth positive results in your life.
559. Exercise the faith that overcomes problems by praying and believing for a change.
560. Prophesy change to every prevailing circumstance you are facing.
561. Pray that the presence of the Lord will convey His blessing anywhere you are.
562. Pray for the grace to overlook the jeers, criticisms and negatives that may come from jealous people.
563. Ask the Lord to help you to be a channel of blessing to other growing Christians in the

name of Jesus.

564. Ask the Lord for the grace to operate with a childlike heart.

565. Receive the grace to walk with a humble heart in everything you do.

566. Take authority over every strongman that is binding you in the name of the Lord.

567. Pray that the entrance of God's Word will bring transformation to your life in Jesus name.

568. Dedicate your body as a temple for the Holy Spirit, asking God for the grace to live in purity.

569. Pull down every stronghold of the mind and every form of imagination that contradicts the message of Christ.

570. Pray that at all times you will only do the perfect will of God.

571. Pray for the grace to overcome whatever will hinder you from entering heaven in Jesus name.

572. Ask for the grace to put the fleshly desires in you under the control of the Holy Spirit.

573. Reject every root of hatred in you and pray that you will flow in the love of God.

574. Thank the Lord for making you a renewed person in Christ.

575. Refuse any condemnation that the enemy tries to use to bind you to the past.

576. Thank the Lord for the light of the Word

enlightening your path from day to day in the name of Jesus.

CONFESSION

I believe and confess that the Lord is good and His grace abounds on to me.

By faith I receive His grace to see transformation in every area of my life. He has taken away hindrances from my way. I pull down the strongholds of the mind and every form of imagination which contradicts the Word of God.

By faith I confess that I overcome fleshly devices and bring them under the subjection of the Holy Spirit. In place of hatred I am filled with the love of God and in place of all darkness the light of the word enlightens my faith.

I am blessed and highly favoured.

CHEERFULN

Psalm 16:11   Nehemiah 12:43   Psalm 9:2
Psalm 19:8   Proverbs 15:13   Isaiah 55:12
Act 27:22   Acts 27:36   2 Corinthians 9:7
James 5:13   1 Peter 1:8

577. Receive the anointing to become a channel of joy.
578. Pray that you will be a channel of God's joy to many generations.
579. Confess that only the shout of joy will be heard in the place of your dwelling.
580. Pray that the seed you have sown in tears will begin to bloom and cause you to rejoice.
581. Pray that in your going out and coming in, you shall increase in your joy.
582. Pray that you will be able to lift up those whose spirits are down.
583. Ask the Lord to lift your spirit in the face of the greatest insult.
584. Pray for the anointing to encourage others in

...me of Jesus.

Come against every cloud of discouragement and worry in the name of the Lord.

586. Pray for the kind of boldness to rejoice in the face of adversity.

587. Thank the Lord for helping you find joy in His presence.

588. Lift up your voice and praise the Lord because He will help you to rejoice at all times.

589. Pray that no matter what you go through, your heart will be filled with the joy of the Lord.

590. Pray that even in the face of adversity, the joy of the Lord shall be your source of joy.

591. Take authority over the things that tend to want to sap your joy and declare that you are full of the joy of the Holy Spirit.

592. Thank God for filling your life with the joy that is inexpressible and glorious in the name of Jesus.

593. Pray that your captivity will be turned around and your impossible situation will turn to a testimony.

594. Ask the Lord to bring to pass your expectation and cause you to rejoice in the name of the Lord.

595. Pray that the entrance of God's Word will bring great delight to your life in the name of Jesus.

596. Thank the Lord for filling you with the peace

and joy produced by the Holy Spirit.

597. Express the joy of the Lord as you sing of God's goodness in your life.

598. Pray that the Lord will fill your heart with a reason to be cheerful in the midst of setback.

599. Pray for the boldness to rejoice in the face of the storms of life.

600. Thank the Lord for the assurance that no matter what you go through He will make a way out.

601. Pray for the grace to be cheerful in your attitude to giving.

602. Pray that you will be a walking message of joy and cheerfulness at all times.

CONFESSION

I believe and confess that my spirit is being lifted up and God causes me to rejoice. In the face of adversity, I receive God's help to find joy in the time of trouble.

In the face of an impossible situation what I face shall turn to a testimony, for the Lord will turn around that which the enemy has stolen to my joy, and He shall fill me with the joy that is unspeakable and glorious. The joy of the Lord which flows from my life shall be a testimony to those who see me.

For I am blessed and highly favoured.

COMFORT

Genesis 24:67
2 Samuel 14:17
Job 6:10
Psalm 77:2
Psalm 119:52
Isaiah 52:9
Isaiah 61:2
Zechariah 1:17
John 14:18
Acts 20:12
1 Corinthians 14:3
2 Corinthians 1:6
2 Corinthians 13:11
Philippians 2:20
Colossians 4:11
1 Thessalonians 3:7
2 Thessalonians 2:16-17

Genesis 37:35
Ruth 2:13
Job 16:2
Psalm 94:19
Psalm 119:76
Isaiah 54:11
Isaiah 66:13
Matthew 5:4
John 14:26
Romans 1:12
1 Corinthians 14:31
2 Corinthians 7:4
Ephesians 6:22
Colossians 2:2
1 Thessalonians 2:11
1 Thessalonians 4:18
1 Peter 3:8

Genesis 38:12
Job 2:11
Psalm 69:20
Psalm 119:50
Ecclesiastes 4:1
Isaiah 57:18
Jeremiah 8:18
Matthew 9:22
Acts 9:31
Romans 15:4
2 Corinthians 1:3-4
2 Corinthians 7:7
Philippians 2:1-2
Colossians 4:8
1 Thessalonians 3:2
1 Thessalonians 5:14

603. Pray for the ability to express godly compassion to people in need.

604. Ask the Lord to strengthen you to show genuine interest in people's need.

605. Ask the Lord to use you to restore not to destroy other people.

606. Pray that you will be comforted with the kind of comfort that will help others.

607. Receive the anointing to bring joy to those who are mourning.

608. Thank the Lord who is the Father of all comforts, for His grace that is sufficient in all situations.

609. Pray that the Lord will comfort you during your grieving moments.

610. Ask the Lord to make you a source of encouragement to those who are mourning.

611. Ask for the grace of God to overcome every situation that has troubled your mind.

612. Come against every tribulation that may have risen against you in the name of the Lord.

613. Ask the Lord to make you an instrument of comfort to those who are in trouble.

614. Ask the Holy Spirit to release God's help for the situations you are facing.

615. Refuse the impact and control of every tendency to walk in worry, in the name of the Lord.

616. Refuse to be controlled by worry and every attack of the enemy on your heart in the name of Jesus.

617. Pray that the Holy Spirit will open your eyes to see the help available to you in the name of Jesus.

618. Pray that the Lord will establish your heart in the midst of your temporary setback.

619. Pray that the mercy of the Lord will bring comfort to your spirit.

620. Pray that in the midst of your affliction, the comfort of the Lord will abound.

621. Thank the Lord for the constant comfort of the Holy Spirit in the midst of setback.

622. Thank God for the comfort derived from the word of God in the midst of setback.

623. Pray that God, the Father of all comforts, will fill your heart with His mercies.

624. Pray that you will know exceeding joy in the midst of tribulation.

625. Pray that the Word of the Lord through you will bring comfort to the hearers.

626. Thank the Lord for the people He has used to minister to you in your down moments.

627. Pray that you will be ministered to through the love of the brethren in your challenging times.

628. Pray that the Lord will open your eyes to see those who need the ministry of comfort around you.

629. Pray that you will overcome grief and receive the comfort of the Lord.

630. In your moments of weakness draw on the comfort which the Holy Spirit brings.

631. Pray that you will always speak a word of comfort to those who have been hurt.

632. Pray that in your challenging times others will bring the comfort you need.

633. Pray that the comfort of the Lord will abound unto His people.

634. Pray that you will be able to reach out with the comfort of the Lord which you have experienced.

635. Ask the Lord to open your eyes to the feeble minded around you and comfort them.

636. Break the hold of the enemy which causes you to refuse comfort in your trouble.

637. Pray for the kind of breakthrough which will bring comfort in your trouble.

638. Pray that the Lord will lead you to the place where you will abound in His comfort.

639. Pray that the favour and comfort of God will be manifest in your life.

640. Delight yourself in the comfort of the Lord when your heart is overwhelmed.

641. Pray that the peace and comfort of the Lord which you lost will return.

642. Thank the Lord for the comfort which the Holy Spirit brings.

643. Pray that the Holy Spirit will come along side to help and lead you in the name of Jesus.

644. Break the hold of the oppressor over your life in the name of the Lord, and receive God's comfort.

645. Ask the Lord to expose those who are miserable comforters around you.

646. Release the power of self-encouragement upon yourself in the name of Jesus.

647. Pray for the boldness to bring God's comfort to those who are grieving.

648. Thank the Lord for the fellowship of His comfort that you share with others.
649. Pray that you will hold on confidently to the prophesy that God will still comfort Zion.

CONFESSION

I bless the name of the Lord, because He is good. I thank the Lord for He hears me when I call Him.

By faith I receive the strength of the Lord who is the Father of all comforts. His grace and power shall be sufficient for me in every situation. He helps me to rise against every tribulation and establishes me in the times of setbacks.

I believe and confess that every grief and worry have lost their grip in the name of Jesus Christ. My life is strengthened to minister to others and to show them the comfort of the Lord.

For I am blessed and highly favoured.

COMMITMENT

Job 14:14   Proverbs 3:5   Matthew 7:7
Matthew 10:22   Luke 9:23-25   1 Corinthians 9:2-5
1 Corinthians 9:27 2 Corinthians 9:25 1 Timothy 6:20
2 Timothy 1:12   2 Timothy 1:14   2 Timothy 4:6
Titus 1:3

650. Receive the anointing to be an achiever, overcomer and a good finisher in the name of Jesus.

651. Ask the Lord to give you the heart of a servant for effective ministry.

652. Thank the Lord for giving you leaders and mentors who watch over your spirit.

653. Pray for the grace to put your all on the altar of sacrifice in the name of Jesus.

654. Pray for the grace to avoid making exceptions when faced with challenges.

655. Take authority over every time consuming distraction of satan and break free from it.

656. Ask for the grace to yield to the Holy Spirit so that your life will always be a challenge to

those around you.

657. Thank Him for seeing you through major and minor challenges of life.

658. Resist everything that wants to stop you from reaching your goal in Jesus name.

659. Ask the Lord to take you beyond good intentions to achievements.

660. Pray that the Lord will help you not to be just busy, but to achieve the vision He has for you.

661. Pray that you will be a committed person in interpersonal relationships.

662. Receive the strength to be devoted and committed to your life assignment.

663. Pray for the grace to face the challenge and be committed to your marriage.

664. Thank the Lord for upholding you by His mighty hand.

665. Pray for the grace to be faithful to the end no matter what comes your way.

666. Ask the Lord to give you the spirit to overcome in all situations.

667. Pray that the journey you started well will also finish well.

668. Ask for the grace to be among those who run this spiritual race in the right way.

669. Reject and refuse every spirit of discouragement in the name of the Lord.

670. Pray for the grace to overcome carnal tendencies that want to drag you back in the

name of Jesus.

671. Confess by faith that you will not go back to the things that seem to draw you away from the perfect will of God.

672. Pray for the grace to let go of anything that wants to stand between you and the Lord.

673. Pray that you will be totally yielded to the will of God for your life.

674. Ask for the strength to give all it takes to succeed in your Christian life.

675. Ask for the grace to give it all it takes in the ministry.

676. Confess by faith that you have laid your hands to the plough and you will not look back.

677. Receive by faith the grace to give it everything to be a success for God.

678. Pray that the Lord will anoint your eyes to see and overcome the tricks of the enemy in the name of Jesus.

679. Pray that no matter what you go through you will be a testimony of God's good works.

680. Ask the Lord for the grace to keep asking until there is a result.

681. Pray for the grace to keep asking until your change comes in the name of the Lord.

682. Pray for the grace to keep asking until there is a result.

CONFESSION

I believe and confess that I am a child of God, committed to doing His will on earth. I receive grace to achieve my goals and visions. I will fulfil my purpose on earth. God's mighty hand upholds me and strengthens me to be faithful to the end.

I reject discouragement, carnal tendency and everything that wants to stop me. My eyes are anointed to see the tricks of the devil and to overcome. I am totally yielded to do the will of God. God has begun a good thing in me and He will equip me to finish well.

I am blessed and highly favoured.

COMPASSION

Exodus 2:6
1 Samuel 23:21
2 Chronicles 30:9
Psalm 28:7
Psalm 111:4
Jeremiah 12:15
Micah 7:19
Matthew 18:27
Luke 15:20
1 Peter 3:8

Deuteronomy 13:17
1 Kings 8:50
2 Chronicles 36:15
Psalm 78:38
Psalm 145:8
Lamentation 3:22
Zechariah 7:9
Matthew 18:33
Romans 9:15
Jude 22

Deuteronomy 30:3
2 Kings 13:23
Psalm 25:2
Psalm 86:15
Isaiah 49:15
Lamentation 3:32
Matthew 9:36
Mark 5:19
Hebrews 10:34

683. Thank the Lord because you will not be put to shame as you trust in Him.

684. Pray that you will find the help of the Lord as you trust in Him.

685. Hold confidently to the prophecy that God will still comfort Zion.

686. Pray for a heart of genuine compassion toward the unsaved friends you have.

687. Thank the Lord for a heart of compassion towards the needy.

688. Thank the Lord for He has not consumed us

THE POWER OF POSITIVE PRAYER

because of His compassion.

689. Pray that the forgiveness and compassion of the Lord will flow to His people from His throne.

690. Thank the Lord for His forgiveness that flows to us because God is full of compassion.

691. Ask the Lord for a heart that is moved with compassion towards others.

692. Praise the Lord for His promise that He shall not retain His anger forever.

693. Pray that you will be surrounded by His mercy and compassion at all times.

694. Thank the Lord for His love and mercy that brought salvation to you.

695. Thank God for providing mercy until mercy has a seat in His temple.

696. Hold on to the promise that your children shall find His compassion in Christ.

697. Pray that the grace that brings salvation will be made known to your friends.

698. Pray that your heart will always be burdened to win souls for Christ and His kingdom.

699. Pray for the kind of compassion that results in ministry to hurting people.

700. Pray that the Lord will bring your way those whom you can show the love of God.

701. Pray that the Lord will lead those who can minister to you, to come your way.

702. Receive the healing of the Lord for those places where you may have been chastised by Him.

703. Receive healing for those areas of your life

where you have been hurt in Jesus name.

704. Pray that you will be a blessing to bring the love of God to those who are in bondage.

705. Pray that the Lord will look on your situation and show His abundant mercy.

706. Ask the Lord to help you to show His love to those who have offended you.

707. Ask the Lord to expose every imminent danger to you in the name of Jesus.

708. Pray that your ministry will flow out of a heart of compassion and mercy.

709. Thank the Lord for the love and mercy that made you to be counted with those of His own.

710. Pray that the compassion of the Lord will flow to you and He will remember His covenant of love.

711. Thank God for His promise to not forget you but remember you and show you His compassion.

712. Pray that the place of your captivity will turn to the place of the manifestation of His compassion.

713. In the midst of people's abandonment and departure from you, pray for the abundant love of God.

714. God said He will show compassion on those He chooses, thank Him for favouring you with love.

715. Ask the Lord to help you not to walk in what will turn away His compassion.

716. Thank the Lord for the restoration of

everything you have lost.

717. Pray that the love of God will flow in the fellowship to which you belong in Jesus name.

718. Pray that nothing will hinder the love of God in your midst.

719. Thank the Lord for you will not be put to shame for depending on Him.

720. Pray that the Lord will teach you to be a repairer of the breach between you and those who have offended you.

721. Thank the Lord for His infinite mercy to those who trust Him.

722. Thank the Lord for the saving power of the gospel of Jesus Christ.

723. Ask the Lord to show you His compassion in the midst of the satanic captivity you are facing.

724. Pray that the favour and compassion of the Lord will be revealed to you even through unsaved people.

725. Repent of anything you know may be hindering the flow of God's compassion.

726. Release your children who have been taken captive because of your disobedience.

727. Pray that the Lord's face of compassion will not be turned away from you.

728. Thank the Lord for His grace that brought salvation when we were yet sinners.

729. Ask the Lord to forgive you of any unconfessed sin that can hinder your prayer.

730. Pray that the mercy and compassion of the Lord

that leads to salvation will be made known to you friends.

731. Pray that the mercy and compassion of the Lord which leads to salvation will be made known to your children.

732. Pray that the mercy and compassion of the Lord which leads to salvation will be made known to your spouse.

733. Thank the Lord for the mercy which He has shown in rescinding His judgement.

734. Pray that the ministry of compassion will flow from you to others in Jesus name.

735. Pray that the anger of the Lord will be turned away from your loved ones and that they will be saved.

736. Pray that you will flow in the compassion of the Lord in the name of Jesus.

737. Pray that you will develop long-suffering and abundant mercy in the name of Jesus.

738. Pray that God's overflowing compassion will bring healing to your community.

739. Pray that the overflowing mercy of God will bring healing to your city.

740. Ask the Lord to burden your heart with the lost condition of the unregenerate.

741. Pray that you will come to understand the true condition of lost men in the name of Jesus.

742. Receive the anointing to bring healing to suffering humanity in the name of Jesus.

743. Ask the Lord to make you an instrument of

His compassion in Jesus name.

744. Ask the Lord to help you to show compassion like Jesus did.

745. Pray that you will reach out to bless those who are less fortunate in the name of Jesus.

746. Pray for a heart of godly compassion to those who have hurt you in the name of Jesus.

747. Ask the Lord to open your eyes to see those who need your ministry.

748. Pray that the Lord will send the kind of help that will draw you out of your troubled waters.

749. Thank the Lord for sending to you those who will fight on your behalf even when absent.

750. Pray that you will not be left in the dark but will be led of the Lord to do the right thing.

751. Thank the Lord in advance for sending help from places and people you do not expect.

752. Receive the compassion of the Lord that will avert any coming danger in your life.

753. Pray that the Lord will send to your life those who will look at your situation with compassion.

754. Receive the healing of the Lord for those areas where He may have brought His judgement in your life.

755. Ask the Lord to deal with all traces of crookedness in your life and character in the name of Jesus.

756. Pray that you will see the loss of friends and be burdened for their salvation.

757. Ask the Lord to help you to show love to

those who do not deserve it.

758. Ask the Lord to help you overcome every tendency to be judgmental.

759. Receive the humility to rejoice at the sight of other people's salvation and blessing.

760. Pray that the Lord will raise more people for neglected ministries like prisons.

761. Pray that the Lord will use you to minister to those who seem to be abandoned.

762. Pray that the words of your mouth will bring deliverance to those who are in bondage.

763. Ask the Lord to help you minister with compassion to those who are doubters.

764. Thank the Lord for remembering His promise concerning the righteous, thus not destroying him.

765. Thank the Lord for His promise never to forget you.

766. Pray that the Lord's compassion will flow in the form of Him remembering you in your situation.

767. In the time of your brokenness, remember the promise of His coming back to heal and deliver you.

768. Thank God for His compassion to you despite what you have done.

769. Share with other people what the compassion of the Lord has done for you.

770. Reflect on the abundant mercy of the Lord and thank Him for it.

771. Receive a tender heart to show compassion like Jesus did to you in the name of Jesus.

772. Pray that the spirit of love and unity will prevail where you worship.

773. Pray that the compassion of the Lord and tenderness will prevail in your midst.

774. Ask the Lord to expose to you what can make you lose His mercy and compassion.

775. Thank the Lord because His compassion will bring you back to the place of His healing.

CONFESSION

I believe and confess that the Lord is good. I thank the Lord for a heart of compassion towards the needy. I give God praise for He has not consumed us because of His compassion. I bless the name of the Lord for providing mercy until mercy has a seat in His temple.

By faith, I confess that forgiveness and compassion will flow to His people from His throne. I boldly confess that God's grace brings salvation to me and to all my friends. The compassion of the Lord will result in ministering to the hurting people. The compassion of the Lord will flow through me and make a way to those who need to know the love of God.

I confess that the Lord will lead those who can

minister to me to come my way. I receive God's mercy and compassion for every situation that I may be in. I speak by faith that the Lord will expose every imminent danger to me in Jesus name. I boldly confess that my ministry will flow out of a heart of compassion and mercy.

I boldly confess that the place of my captivity will turn to the place of the manifestation of God's compassion and in the midst of peoples abandonment and departure from me, I will know the abundance of God's love. I bless the name of the Lord for He has promised not to forget me or forsake me. I thank the Lord because nothing will hinder His love to me.

I give God praise for the restoration of everything which I have lost.

I am blessed and highly favoured.

CONCENTRATION

Matthew 7:7-8   John 9:4   Roman 15:20
1 Corinthians 9:24 Philippians 3:14   Philippians 4:13
Hebrews 10:35

776. Receive the grace to always dwell on the promises of God and not the greatness of the circumstance.

777. Ask the Lord to give you the heart of a servant for effective ministry.

778. Take authority over every time consuming distraction of satan and break free from it.

779. Ask the Lord to help you so that you are not led astray by earthly guides.

780. Thank the Lord for His grace and calling.

781. Give God the praise for His continuous leading in your life.

782. Pray for the grace to major on the programme of God for your life.

783. Ask the Lord to help you locate His programme for your life and the grace to pursue it.

784. Pray that the Holy Spirit will help you to forget

the mistakes of the past in the name of the Lord.

785. Take authority over every destructive element in your life and command such elements to depart in the name of the Lord.

786. Confess your choice of happiness in the midst of setback in the name of the Lord.

787. Pray for the grace to focus on the goals of your life and not the distractions of the enemy.

788. Confess that by faith you will rise to your destined calling in the name of the Lord.

789. Ask the Lord for the grace to give the little talent you have to the Lord for Him to increase.

790. Take authority over every tendency to drift into worry and anxiety.

791. Ask the Lord for the grace to push on to possess your possession in the name of the Lord.

792. Pray that the Lord will help you to keep your eyes on finishing the race you already began.

793. Ask the Lord to help you be wise with the time and talent He has given you in the name of the Lord.

794. Thank the Lord for strength to achieve His plans for your life in the name of Jesus.

795. Come against the spirit of discouragement in the face of unanswered prayer.

796. Refuse to succumb to every attempt of the enemy to make you give up before your breakthrough comes in the name of the Lord.

CONFESSION

I give God the praise for His continuous leading in my life. I thank the Lord for helping me to locate His programme for my life.

God gives me the grace to forget the mistakes of the past and every evil destructive element. I receive boldness to be happy in the midst of setback and overcome the spirit of discouragement.

I boldly confess that I am focused on my goals. I have received grace to possess my possession. I keep my eyes on finishing the race as I arise to my destiny and calling.

I am blessed and highly favoured.

CONFIDENCE

Psalm 27:3   Psalm 118:8-9   Micah 7:5
Matthew 10:32   Romans 2:18-19   Romans 12:12
2 Corinthians 5:6   2 Corinthians 5:8 Ephesians 6:14-18
Philippians 1:6   Philippians 1:14   Philippians 4:13

797. Declare that the enemy is under your feet and tread upon him and his works.
798. Receive grace from the Lord to stand tall in trouble times.
799. Confess your ability to do all things through Christ who strengthens you.
800. Thank the Lord for the strength and confidence that comes through moments of quietness.
801. Thank the Lord for the grace and favour which comes through the knowledge of Him.
802. Pray for the confidence and boldness to share Jesus Christ with people.
803. Ask the Lord to give you the grace to tell the world of His saving grace.

804. Confess that every mouth that rises against you in judgement shall be condemned.

805. Refuse to be bound by the spirit of *"the fear of men"* in the name of Jesus.

806. Boldly take authority over the attacks of the enemy and declare your victory in the name of the Lord.

807. Thank God for the promise He gave that anything you bind or loose, will be as you declared in the name of Jesus.

808. Pray for the spirit of boldness and confidence in your prayer life.

809. Pray for the confidence to stand in the times of setback in the name of Jesus.

810. Take authority over every fiery arrow of the enemy in the name of Jesus.

811. Tear down every wall the enemy is building against, trying to limit you in the work of the Lord.

812. Ask the Lord for the spirit of perseverance in prayer in the name of the Lord.

813. Ask the Lord for the grace to persevere until your results comes in the name of the Lord.

814. Pray that the victorious work God started in your life will be accomplished in the name of Jesus.

815. Pray that the Lord will execute the downfall of satan in your life in the name of Jesus.

816. Ask the Lord for the confidence to run the Christian race in the name of the Lord.

817. Confess by faith that your vision will come to

pass in the name of the Lord.

818. Thank the Lord for His ability that dwells in you and helps you to face all situations.

819. Confess by faith that you will be further ahead tomorrow than you are today in the name of Jesus.

820. Pray that you will be filled with the confidence of the Lord every day.

CONFESSION

I believe and confess that the grace and favour of the Lord abounds to me. God gives me the confidence and boldness to be a witness for Him. Anything I bind or loose shall be as I declare, in Jesus name. I have the authority of God over the attacks of the enemy. I refuse to be bound by the spirit of fear of men.

I boldly declare that I shall stand in the times of setbacks and overcome the arrows of the enemy until my change comes.

By faith, I declare that every wall the enemy places against me crumbles, in the name of Jesus. I shall see the downfall of satan and live in total victory throughout my Christian race.

I am blessed and highly favoured.

CONSECRATION

Exodus 29:37   1 Chronicles 29:5   2 Chronicles 29:5
Psalm 15:1-2   Isaiah 29:23   Daniel 4:9
Romans 12:1-2   2 Corinthians 7:1   1 Timothy 2:8
2 Timothy 1:9   1 Peter 2:9   2 Peter 3:11
1 John 1:7   1 John 1:9

821. Receive the anointing to be an achiever, overcomer and a good finisher in the name of Jesus.

822. Thank the Lord for giving you leaders and mentors who watch over your spirit.

823. Thank the Lord for the spirit of grace and holiness.

824. Pray that you will receive grace to live a holy life.

825. Make a commitment today to consecrate your life to the Lord.

826. Pray that you will be a useful vessel to the Lord.

827. Thank the Lord for counting you worthy to be part of His holy people.

828. Pray for the grace to consecrate a time and place to meet and worship the Lord.

829. Receive help by faith from the Holy Spirit, so that your walk and talk will be holy.

830. Thank God for counting you worthy to be among His chosen generation.

831. Pray that at all times you will learn to hallow and honour the name of the Lord.

832. Pray that you will be a carrier of the spirit of the Lord.

833. Ask the Lord for the grace to keep your body from all kinds of *"flesh sin"*.

834. Pray that the Lord will give you a new mind, which is influenced by the Holy Spirit.

835. Ask the Holy Spirit to help you to be holy in all your conduct.

836. Thank the Lord who has called you with a holy calling.

837. Reject every tendency and sin that wants to draw you away from the will of God.

838. Pray that your life will be a testimony of holy living in a world of compromise.

839. Loose yourself from all the things that tend to bind you in the name of the Lord.

840. Declare your freedom from the bondage of sin, in the name of the Lord.

841. Pray you will walk in the fear and reverence of the Lord at all times.

842. Ask the Lord to cleanse your heart with His precious blood.

843. Pray for the grace to walk in the light of the Word at all times.

844. Ask the Lord to cleanse you from all unrighteousness.

845. Thank the Lord for forgiving your past and guaranteeing your future.

846. Receive the grace to serve the Lord with sensitivity of heart.

847. Receive the grace to walk in godly repentance from all known sin.

848. Pray that at all times you will walk in humility before God.

CONFESSION

I believe and confess that the Lord is good. His faithfulness endures forever. I receive His grace to live a godly life. I am committed to live for Jesus. By faith I receive the ability to live victorious in the face of temptation.

I boldly confess that all that I do will bring honour to the name of the Lord. My body is yielded to the service of the Lord. My mind is renewed by the Word of God. The Holy Spirit lives in me. Sin has no dominion over me. I have a testimony of holy living. I am free from spiritual bondage to serve the Lord with a godly heart.

I am blessed and highly favoured.

COURAGE

Numbers 13:20   Deuteronomy 7:23   Deuteronomy 31:6
Joshua 1:7   Joshua 2:11   Joshua 23:6
1 Chronicles 28:20   2 Chronicles 15:8   2 Chronicles 19:11
2 Chronicles 32:7   Psalm 27:14   Psalm 30:6
Psalm 31:24   Isaiah 41:6   Acts 28:15
1 Corinthians 16:13

849. Ask the Lord to renew your strength and prepare you for any coming battle.

850. Receive freedom from a defeatist spirit and walk in boldness.

851. Receive the boldness to stand against whatever is against your prosperity.

852. Thank the Lord who gives you the courage to win in all situations.

853. Give God praise because He started a good work in you and will complete it.

854. Pray for the courage to face the challenges you are facing in your life.

855. Bind the spirit of fear from controlling your life in the name of the Lord.

856. Take authority over the plan of the enemy and declare your victory ahead in the name of the Lord.

857. Pray that the presence of the Lord will go with you everywhere you are in the name of Jesus.

858. Thank the Lord for His promise to stand by you and not forsake you.

859. Pray for the boldness to possess your possession.

860. Pray for the boldness to take back that which the enemy has stolen.

861. Hold on to the promise of God in the face of any challenge and declare that it shall be well.

862. Boldly confess that you will enter and possess that which the Lord has earmarked for you in the name of the Lord.

863. Thank the Lord because He will be there for you in times of trials.

864. Come against every spirit of fear and confusion of mind in the name of the Lord.

865. Ask for the ability to discern the strategies of the enemy in the name of Jesus.

866. Thank the Lord for the courage to stand in the face of overwhelming temptations.

867. Pray for the courage to say no to the subtle lies of the enemy in the name of Jesus.

868. Pray for the grace to withstand the arrows of your enemies in the name of Jesus.

869. Take authority over every intimidation of satan and declare your victory in advance.

870. Pray for the courage and strength to finish your

race well.

871. Confess by faith that even in your weakness you are strong.

872. Ask the Lord for the grace to act courageously in the face of challenges.

873. Ask the Lord to strengthen you so you will not be afraid of an opposing multitude.

874. Reject every intimidation of those who are high and mighty in the name of Jesus.

875. Thank the Lord for the host of angels who are more than those who are against you in the name of the Lord.

876. Thank the Lord for the continuous dosage of courage in the face of challenges.

877. Pray for the boldness to confront the enemy and take back what has been stolen from you.

878. Receive courage in the fact that the Lord goes before you to give you victory.

879. Receive the strengthening of the Lord that leads to courage in Jesus name.

880. Pray for the boldness to carry out the daunting goals and projects you have.

881. Pray for the boldness to reach forth and possess your possession.

882. Boldly tear down any idol in your life that may have risen against the glory of God.

883. Rejoice because they that be for you are more than your enemies.

884. Pray for the boldness to confront and overcome your worst enemy.

885. Pray for the boldness to confront the challenges that have come against you.
886. Pray for the courage to live a godly life in a godless world.
887. Ask for the courage to do what the Word of God says and not what the situation dictates.
888. Thank the Lord for the courage to know that the battle is not over until you win.
889. Thank the Lord for His grace in the face of every discouraging experience in the name of Jesus.
890. Pray for the boldness and courage to withstand your greatest opposition in the name of the Lord.

CONFESSION

I believe and confess that the Lord gives me courage to overcome every challenge I face.

I declare that the presence of the Lord goes with me into all situations. The promise of the Lord is good for me, no matter what I face, and the grace of the Lord strengthens me everyday.

I boldly take back what the enemy has stolen, because my eyes are anointed to see the strategies of the enemy and to say no to the subtle lies of satan.

I believe and confess that I shall act

courageously in the face of challenges, for the Lord will go before me to win all my battles. They that are for me are greater than those who are against me for the battle is not over until I win.

I am blessed and highly favoured.

DECISION

Deuteronomy 30:19   2 Chronicles 2:1   Job 14:5
Proverbs 11:14   Proverbs 16:33   Proverbs 24:6
Acts 2:23   Acts 4:28   Acts 5:38
Acts 17:26   1 Corinthians 2:2 1 Corinthians 4:5
Ephesians 1:11   Hebrews 6:17   1 Peter 5:10

891. Thank the Lord for perfecting, establishing and strengthening you at all times.

892. Thank the Lord for directing your path daily.

893. Give God the praise for helping you to find His favour daily.

894. Ask the Lord to open your eyes to know the programmes you have which are not from Him.

895. Pray that every counsel taken against your well being will not stand in the name of the Lord.

896. Pray that your choices will glorify the Lord.

897. Ask the Lord to guide your mind to make decisions that will lead to life.

898. Bind every spirit of confusion that may want

to attack you.

899. At the crossroads of life reject every manifestation of confusion in the name of Jesus.

900. Bind the spirit of procrastination and receive the anointing for wise action.

901. Pray that the counsel of the Lord concerning your life will be established.

902. Ask the Lord to anoint your eyes to know time wasting decisions, jobs etc.

903. Pray that actions will be wise and that you will be led of the Lord at all times.

CONFESSION

I believe and confess that the Lord is good and He directs my path daily. The Lord is on my side and He opens my eyes to know His ways.

I boldly confess that God anoints my mind to make good decisions. Every counsel taken against my wellbeing shall not stand, for my eyes shall be anointed to know time-wasting decisions and to reject procrastination.

I give God praise for I shall be led by Him at all times.

I am blessed and highly favoured.

DELIVERANCE

Genesis 45:7   Numbers 31:5   Deuteronomy 27:16-26
Judges 15:18   2 Kings 13:17   Ezra 9:13
Psalm 18:50   Psalm 22:5   Psalm 32:7
Psalm 44:4   Proverbs 11:8-9   Proverbs 11:21
Isaiah 54:14-17   Isaiah 49:25   Joel 2:32
Obadiah 17

904. Come against the spirit of spiritual slumber in the name of Jesus.

905. Jesus gave power over serpents; take authority over every serpentine spirit and declare your victory over them.

906. Stand on God's Word which says you shall trample on the dragon.

907. Thank God for His faithfulness to deliver His children from the onslaught of the enemy.

908. Cast out every demonic squatter from your life in the name of the Lord.

909. Plead the blood of Jesus against the molestation of the devil in all areas of your life.

910. Repent and ask the Holy Spirit to cleanse your heart from every kind of lewdness.

911. Receive deliverance from the bondage of depression in the name of the Lord.

912. Thank the Lord for setting you free from tendencies of a desperate spirit.

913. Pray that you will be free from an unhealthy competitive spirit in the name of the Lord.

914. Humble yourself before the Lord and be free from the tendency to be confrontational.

915. Cover yourself with the blood of Jesus against every seductive spirit.

916. Thank the Lord in advance for setting you free from the bondage of uncontrollable jealousy.

917. Repent on behalf of your city for the sins that can bring the judgement of God.

918. Pray against the rise of the religion of evil and satan worship in the name of Jesus.

919. Break the hold of every evil pronouncement made into your life in the past in Jesus name.

920. Destroy every impending trouble even before it arises in the name of the Lord.

921. Ask the Lord for the grace to stay away from the associations that are not helping your spiritual progress.

922. Take authority over every lie of satan perpetrated against you and declare that they shall have no effect in the name of the Lord.

923. Give God the glory for His deliverance from every trap of the enemy.

924. Thank the Lord who always causes you to have victory in the Lord.

925. Take authority over every weapon of bondage in the lives of the members of your family.

926. Release every blessing of the Lord which the enemy is trying to hinder.

927. Take authority over every ancestral spirit working against your family in the name of the Lord.

928. Confess that the Lord will show His great deliverance in your life.

929. Thank the Lord because His mercy will be manifest in your life as His anointed.

930. Ask the Lord to command His deliverance in your life.

931. Confess in the midst of your setback that you will still sing of God's deliverance.

932. Take authority over every trouble the enemy is putting together and nullify it in the name of the Lord.

933. Break the hold of every generational curse on your future in the name of the Lord.

934. Cancel the impact of every family curse to the tenth generation.

935. Pray that the Lord will use you as a source of deliverance to those in bondage.

936. Cancel every seed which the enemy may have planted in your life through previous sexual entanglements.

937. Thank the Lord for the great deliverance He wrought despite your mistake.

938. Pray that God's deliverance power will flow from your church to those in bondage.

939. Pray that His mighty power will loose you from the control of satan.

940. Confess that according to the Word of God you will possess your blessing.

941. Pray that you will continue to be used for the ministry of setting people free.

942. Pray that the arrow of the Lord's deliverance will vindicate you.

943. Release the arrow of deliverance against every satanic attack.

944. Give God the glory because He wrought a great victory in your life.

945. Stand on God's promise to deliver you because you have chosen to walk in righteousness.

946. Ask the Lord to give you the divine insight that leads to deliverance.

947. Cover your children with the blood of Jesus.

948. Break the hold of every satanic bondage over your children in the name of the Lord

949. Thank the Lord because He will cause you to know His deliverance amidst thousands.

950. Pray that your cry of deliverance will not go unheeded.

951. Break yourself free from the power of the evil one.

952. Break the curse of worshipping any ungodly image in your family.

953. Break the curse of disrespect for family militating against your family.
954. Break the curse of offence committed against your neighbour dating back to generations.
955. Break the curse which comes as a result of misleading the disabled.
956. Break the curse which comes as a result of offence against a foreigner.
957. Break the impact of the curse of incest in your family in the name of Jesus.
958. Break the curse of participating in sexual sin in Jesus name.
959. Break the curse which comes as a result of bestiality.
960. Break the curse which comes with committing sin with your in-laws.
961. Break the power of the curse which comes as a result of damaging your neighbours behind their backs.
962. Break the generational curse which follows destroying the innocent without reason.
963. Break the curse which follows disobedience to the Word of God.
964. Breaking the curse which may have come on your business and your income.
965. Cover your children with the blood of Jesus and declare them safe in the Lord.

CONFESSION

I believe and confess that the Lord is good, for I am delivered from the trap of the enemy. The Son of God sets me free and I am free indeed. No evil befalls me. No weapon formed against me prospers.

Every arrow of satan falls for my sake, and every bondage of the devil is cancelled, in Jesus name. The curse from idolatry is broken in my life. The curse from generation sins is broken, in Jesus name.

Christ has redeemed me from the curse of the law. I am free from the power of the evil one. My freedom is guaranteed in Jesus. I am covered by His precious blood.

I am blessed and highly favoured.

DIFFICULT PEOPLE

Exodus 7:14	Nehemiah 2:10	2 Samuel 17:7
Nehemiah 6:1-19	Daniel 6:4-5	Daniel 6:24
Acts 13:6-10	Acts 19:13-17	Ephesians 1:22
Revelation 12:11		

966. Ask the Lord to expose to you, those who are putting on a false zeal around you.

967. Ask the Lord to expose all those who are agents of satan around you.

968. Ask the Lord to expose those who are there to hurt your work.

969. Thank the Lord for His promise to put the enemy under our feet shortly.

970. Take authority over every stronghold of satan and destroy every demonic work in the name of Jesus.

971. Pray that God will shut the mouth of those who oppose the Word of God in your community.

972. Pray for the strength to walk away from those

who put down your vision.

973. Pray for the grace to overlook the jeers, criticisms and negatives that may come from jealous people.

974. Ask the Lord for the grace to stay away from the associations that are not helping your spiritual progress.

975. Thank the Lord for putting down every Pharaoh that wants to hold you to shame in the name of Jesus.

976. Thank the Lord for plundering the path of evil counsellors and defeating the plan of evil judges.

977. Break the hold of the abusive people you know in your life.

978. Ask the Lord to help you to handle people who disrespect your feelings.

979. Ask the Lord to expose any disloyal persons in your establishment in the name of Jesus.

980. Pray that the Lord will expose any person who is dishonest around you in the name of Jesus.

981. Pray for the wisdom to overcome those who deal with you in hatred.

982. Break the hold of the spirit of the fear of man in the name of Jesus.

983. Ask the Lord to help you gain victory over difficult people.

984. Receive boldness to confront those who deliberately frighten people.

985. Pray for the humility to handle those who always bulldoze their way into your affairs.

986. Thank the Lord in advance for the wisdom to handle bossy people.
987. Pray for the grace to avoid the tendency to be brash and uncaring.
988. Pray for your friends who are brazen in their behaviour that they will show the compassion of Christ.
989. Ask the Lord for the wisdom to handle those who are unnecessarily demanding.
990. Pray that you will learn from your dealings with difficult people.
991. Pray that the Holy Spirit will open your eyes to know those who are fake.
992. Pray for the wisdom to handle those who are fake without being polluted.
993. Receive the grace not to walk with those who have a fault-finding spirit.
994. Break the spirit of bickering and quarrels in the lives of your friends.
995. Pray for the wisdom to handle those who are always blaming others for their problems.
996. Ask the Lord to expose anyone who is back stabbing you.
997. Pray that the Lord will expose all the false brethren in your church.
998. Break the hold of the person who belittles your life and vision.
999. Pray that the counsel of the person who constantly attacks you will not stand.
1000. Cover yourself with the blood of Jesus against

the critical spirit that operates against you.

1001. Thank the Lord for the wisdom to handle the person who has an arrogant spirit.

1002. Pray that you will be free from anyone who has been abusive to you.

1003. Ask the Lord to give you wisdom to handle aggressive people.

1004. Pray for the grace to walk in love with those who have acrimony against you.

1005. Thank the Lord for exposing all the conspirators who are against you.

1006. Pray that the Lord will frustrate the efforts of those who are conniving against you.

1007. Pray for the wisdom to handle those who jealously compete with you.

1008. Pray that those who have been unfriendly towards you will begin to change.

1009. Ask the Lord to touch your spouse who seems to be stingy in the name of the Lord.

1010. Receive deliverance from those who are "users" of other people.

1011. Pray that the Lord will touch the heart of your child who is stubborn.

1012. Receive freedom from those who have been unreasonable towards you.

1013. Pray for the wisdom to handle those who are jealous of your success and blessing.

1014. Humble yourself and ask for the grace to deal with irritating people.

1015. Bind the hold of a rebellious spirit over the

people you know.

1016. Thank the Lord in advance for the wisdom to handle those who are loud.

1017. Ask the Lord for the wisdom not to yield to those who are manipulative.

1018. Ask the Lord to expose those who are dealing with you in hypocrisy.

1019. Thank the Lord for touching the heart of those who have been unfriendly to you.

CONFESSION

I believe and confess that God is good. His faithfulness extends to the heavens. I give God praise because He gives me wisdom to handle people who are difficult. I bless the name of the Lord for giving me victory over every satanic lie.

I confess by faith that the dishonest are exposed and that those who mean evil against my life are exposed by the Holy Spirit. I am free from the fear of man. I am victorious over impossible people.

By faith I receive boldness to confront those who deliberately cause fear and panic. I reject the works of the enemy and confess that I have received wisdom to handle those who make unnecessary demands on my life. I have received wisdom to deal with the difficult, for the spirit of the Lord anoints my eyes to see the fake and the truthful.

My eyes are anointed to see the plans of the enemy. My heart is filled with wisdom to handle every situation. No evil, danger or weapon formed against me prospers for the Lord exposes everyone who betrays and false brethren. Those who belittle me shall see me make progress.

The blood of Jesus covers me against every critical spirit, against every spirit of jealousy and against every conspirator who is against me. By faith I confess that I am victorious and everything I touch and do will carry the mark of God's blessing.

I am blessed and highly favoured.

DILIGENCE

Proverbs 4:23 Proverbs 10:4 Proverbs 12:24
Proverbs 12:27 Proverbs 13:4 Proverbs 15:19
Proverbs 19:15 Proverbs 21:5 Proverbs 21:25
Proverbs 22:13 Proverbs 22:29 Proverbs 24:30
Proverbs 26:13-14 Proverbs 27:23 Ecclesiastes 10:18
Act 18:25 Romans 12:8 Romans 12:11
1 Corinthians 9:27 2 Corinthians 8:7 1 Timothy 2:8
2 Peter 1:10

1020. Ask the Lord to help you to be a good finisher of what you start.

1021. Pray against every tendency of laziness in your work or business.

1022. Come against every tendency to regress in your work or business.

1023. Ask the Lord to help you to be watchful in your Christian walk.

1024. Pray that you will not be moved to do wrong when people in the faith disappoint you.

1025. Ask the Lord for the strength to be diligent and productive in the name of Jesus.

1026. Pray that you will know the timing and seasons of God for your life.

1027. Ask the Lord to use the things you are going through to produce a higher dimension of faith.

1028. Thank God for the ability to endure hardness as a good soldier of Jesus Christ.

1029. Pray that the Word of God will speak to you and direct your path so that you will not fail or falter.

1030. Confess by faith that you have laid your hands to the plough and you will not look back.

1031. Pray for the grace to overcome carnal tendencies that want to drag you back in the name of Jesus.

1032. Reject every tendency and sin that wants to raw you away from the will of God.

1033. Thank the Lord for teaching your hand to war and your heart to work.

1034. Give the Lord praise for His promise to prosper the works of your hand.

1035. Command that every hindrance to your progress should give way.

1036. Break yourself free from every tendency of laziness in the name of the Lord.

1037. Deliver yourself by faith from every inordinate desire in the name of Jesus.

1038. Refuse every excuse for failure and declare your commitment to winning.

1039. Pray for the grace to be diligent in every

aspect of your life and reject the spirit of negligence.

1040. Pray that every obstacle in your way will be turned to a stepping stone.

1041. Pray for the motivation to overcome complacency in Jesus name.

1042. Break yourself loose from spiritual slumber which makes one miss His destiny.

1043. Pray that the success you have experienced will not stop but increase.

1044. Reject and refuse every kind of satanic slavery in the name of the Lord.

1045. Pray that you will always complete the projects you start.

1046. Thank the Lord because He will make diligence to be the mark of your life.

1047. Bind every tendency to be sluggish from operating in your life.

1048. Confess by faith that you will, through faith and patience, possess your possessions.

1049. Thank the Lord for fervency and zeal to accomplish your vision.

1050. Pray that the Lord will put His blessing on your diligent labour.

1051. Thank the Lord because His Word already declares you as the head and not the tail.

1052. Receive the anointing to flow in creative thinking in the name of Jesus.

1053. Thank the Lord for His promise to prosper you as you pursue your God-given vision.

1054. Prophesy by faith that the abilities of God in you will open doors for you.

1055. Pray for the grace to be diligent and accountable for the blessings of God.

1056. Receive the grace to lead and guide others with diligence.

1057. Ask the Lord to help you be diligent in the protection of your heart from that which is not profitable.

1058. Pray for the grace to pursue brotherly love with diligence.

1059. Ask God for the grace to be diligent in your proclamation of the gospel.

1060. Ask for the grace to be a diligent teacher of the word of God.

1061. Pray for the wisdom and direction to prove God's call on your life.

1062. Receive by faith the grace to operate in the spirit of diligence and excellence.

CONFESSION

I believe and confess that the Lord is good. He teaches my hand to war and keeps His faithful promises to prosper me. I am anointed to operate in diligence and overcome complacency. Success attends whatever I do. I shall complete everything I start. I take authority over every work of satan and reject his bondage.

I believe and confess that I am fervent and zealous in the Lord. The grace to pursue and possess the blessing of the Lord operates through me.

I am blessed and highly favoured.

DIVINE ACCELERATION

Genesis 15:1   Genesis 16: 10   Genesis 17:2
Genesis 17:6   Genesis 30:43   Exodus 1:7
Numbers 14:7   1 Samuel 20:41   1 Kings 4:29
1 Kings 10:7   1 Kings 10:23   1 Chronicles 22:5
2 Chronicles 9:6   2 Chronicles 32:27   Psalm 21:6
Ezekiel 37:10   2 Corinthians 4:17   Ephesians 1:19
Ephesians 3:20

1063. Give God the praise for His faithfulness at all times.

1064. Thank the Lord for His plan for your life and rejoice in advance for the fulfilment.

1065. Like Elijah pray for the divine ability to overtake those who have gone ahead.

1066. Pray for the anointing to catch up and overtake in the areas of your calling.

1067. Thank the Lord because your victory shall not be by power or by might.

1068. Receive the anointing that came upon Elijah and caused him to outrun chariots.

1069. Confess that like Joseph you are coming out

of the prison of limitation.

1070. Pray for the promotion that leads from prison to palace.

1071. Thank the Lord for fulfilling the dreams He has put in your heart.

1072. Pray for the presence of the Lord on your life which will cause others to promote you.

1073. Joseph's life changed by one appointment with the Pharaoh; pray for such promotion.

1074. Joseph's promotion was manifest in such a way that his brother could not recognise him; pray for a life transforming breakthrough.

1075. Pray for the kind of breakthrough that cancels the pain of the past.

1076. Pray for the kind of breakthrough that will less your future generation.

1077. The life of the prodigal son was changed totally when he encountered the father's love; pray for such a breakthrough.

1078. Thank the Lord for the accelerated breakthrough that will make you recover wasted years.

1079. Pray that your latter days like Job will be greater than the former.

1080. Prophesy a turnaround to the adverse situation you are facing right now.

1081. Begin to prophesy a divine acceleration to the change you expect in the area of adversity in your life.

1082. Receive a divine restoration to the area where

you have experienced a setback.

1083. Thank the Lord for moving on the people He will use to prosper you.

1084. Like David pray for the Lord's strategy for divine acceleration.

1085. Reach forth and take back your property which was stolen by the enemy in the name of Jesus.

1086. Begin to confess by faith that you will recover all that the enemy stole.

1087. Pray that the Lord will hasten your move so that you overtake those who are trying to put you down.

1088. Pray for the accelerated breakthrough of the plough man overtaking the reaper.

1089. Thank the Lord for the day when the treader of grapes will overtake seed sowers.

1090. Pray that the days when harvest will meet harvest will be manifest in your life.

1091. Pray that you will catch up on and overtake those who have taken advantage of you.

1092. Ask the Lord to bring confusion to the camp of the enemy that is pursuing you to destroy you.

1093. Ask the Lord to blow the wind of judgement on the camp of those who are pursuing you without cause.

1094. Ask the Lord to accelerate your speed away from the arrow of those who want your soul.

1095. Cancel every curse that may want to have its effect upon your life with the blood of Jesus.

1096. Confess that according to the Word of God you shall possess everything you pursue.

1097. Thank the Lord because the enemy who continues to pursue you shall be frustrated by the Lord.

1098. Give God praise because He will always put you head of every opposition.

1099. Repent of the sin that may bring divine regression to your life.

1100. Ask the Lord to strengthen you to pursue and not look back until you achieve the victory.

1101. Prophesy that there will be an accelerated achievement on the project you are pursuing.

1102. Prophesy that there will be an accelerated achievement on the destiny of your children.

1103. Prophesy that you will achieve things beyond your dreams and hope, according to His power in you.

1104. Thank the Lord for His promise to do more than you ask or think according to His power in you.

CONFESSION

I believe and confess that God's divine ability works in my life and causes me to overtake those who have gone ahead. I confess that the anointing to catch up and overtake in all areas of calling is upon my life. My victory shall not be by power nor by might, for the Lord who caused Elijah to outrun chariots shall cause me to accelerate in my victory and blessings.

I confess that like Joseph, I am coming out of the prison of humiliation and limitation into the palaces of promotion and elevation. I believe and confess that my dreams are coming to pass for the Lord will cause others to promote me even as He promotes me.

I boldly confess that my blessings shall be manifest for all to see. The spirit of the Lord rests upon my life bringing transformation. The spirit of the Lord rests upon my life and causes the breakthrough that breaks and cancels the pain of the past; the kind of breakthrough that will bless my future generation.

I believe and confess that my latter days shall be greater that the former for the Lord will cause a turnaround to the adverse situation I am facing right now. I prophesy divine acceleration to the change I expect in areas of adversity in my life. I speak forth divine restoration to the areas where I have experienced a setback for the Lord Himself will hasten a move that shall overtake all that has put me down and all that has left me behind.

Breakthrough comes into my life and causes the ploughman to overtake the reaper. For the day of the Lord is upon me, when the treader of grapes will overtake seed sowers. My days of harvest are here. My greatest days are around the corner.

My time of promotion is on hand for the Lord will cause me to possess everything that the enemy stole.

I am blessed and highly favoured.

DIVINE ELEVATION

Exodus 11:3	1 Samuel 2:1	1 Samuel 2:10
Nehemiah 1:11	Nehemiah 9:5	Job 5:11
Psalm 37:34	Psalm 75:10	Psalm 89:17
Psalm 89:19	Psalm 92:10	Psalm 112:9
Proverbs 11:11	Isaiah 30:18	Isaiah 33:10
Daniel 1:8-9	Matthew 23:12	Luke 18:14
Acts 13:17	2 Corinthians 10:5	2 Corinthians 11:7
Philippians 2:9	James 1:9	1 Peter 5:6

1105. Pray that those who are expecting harm to come your way will be surprised by your promotion.

1106. Receive the favour of divine elevation in the sight of the enemy.

1107. Thank the Lord because He will prosper you in the sight of God and man.

1108. Ask the Lord to expose anyone who may be hindering your promotion.

1109. Confess by faith that despite your educational, financial and physical setback, you will make it.

1110. Thank the Lord for the favour of His presence in your life.

1111. Thank God for His steadfast love which never fails at all times.

1112. Thank the Lord for loving you and lifting you out of the dust of defeat.

1113. Pray that the Lord who lifts out of the dust will bring His promotion to your life.

1114. Ask the Lord to break the cycle of degradation in your life in the name of Jesus.

1115. Thank the Lord for making you sit with Him in the heavenly places in Christ.

1116. Pray that the promotion of the Lord in your life will move you from barrenness to fruitfulness

1117. Command that every pit that the enemy dug for you will become your stepping stone.

1118. Confess that you will prosper like Joseph even in the midst of adversity.

1119. Pray that the Lord will bring into your life, those who believe in your ability.

1120. Pray that the gifts in you will make room for you before those who have the capacity to bless you.

1121. Pray that you will be a testimony of God's promotion, like Joseph.

1122. Receive the anointing to operate in a higher dimension of the wisdom of God.

1123. Like Joseph, pray for the kind of promotion that will take you from prison to palace.

1124. Receive God's divine endorsement in your life in the name of Jesus.

1125. Prophesy that the day of the manifestation of your promotion is here in Jesus name.

1126. Pray that you will know the purpose of God for your life and pursue it.

1127. Pray that like Daniel you will manifest the anointing of excellence.

1128. Ask the Lord to help you exhibit the knowledge of the deeper things of God.

1129. Thank the Lord because the wisdom of God manifested in you will confound the wise of this world.

1130. Pray that at all times the Lord will lift you above the wild jealousy of the enemy.

1131. Pray that you will be free from the temptation of self-exaltation.

1132. Pray that you will not walk in pride but give all glory to Jesus for His blessings in your life.

1133. Confess that your hand shall be lifted to possess the land.

1134. Pray that in the face of adversity, your horn of strength shall be exalted.

1135. Pray for the promotion of the Lord which singles out and lifts up.

1136. Receive your breakthrough that will distinguish you among thousands in the name of the Lord.

1137. Thank the Lord for His promotion and His hand of fresh power on your life.

1138. Pray that the blessing of the Lord will not make you walk in foolishness and pride.

1139. Receive the grace to humble yourself and

receive the Lord's elevation.

1140. Like Israel, receive the Lord's promotion even in a foreign land in Jesus name.

1141. Receive the grace to see others lifted up and rejoice with them.

1142. Receive the grace from the Holy Spirit to wait for our season of promotion.

1143. Break yourself free from the carnal tendency to be in haste in the name of the Lord.

1144. Thank the Lord for lifting your head out of the ash of people's humiliation.

1145. Pray that the divine elevation God is bringing to your life will result in promotion of the people of God.

1146. Receive the elevation that honours the Lord in the name of Jesus.

1147. Praise the Lord because the enemy shall not be exalted above you.

1148. Thank the Lord for exalting your horn of honour in the name of Jesus.

1149. Pray the promotion of the Lord in your life shall bring His blessing on your city.

1150. Ask the Lord to use you in His vineyard to bless other believers.

1151. Thank the Lord for His promise to lift righteous people in your community.

1152. Confess that you are coming out of your sadness into a time of rejoicing.

1153. In your lowly status rejoice because you are already lifted in Christ Jesus.

1154. Thank the Lord because the future is as bright as His promises to you.

CONFESSION

I believe and confess that the favour of the Lord is in my life, the steadfast love of the Lord never fails. At all times, He is loving me and lifting me out of the dust of defeat. He has brought me into a place of promotion.

By faith, I confess that the cycle of degradation is broken in my life. For the Lord has made me sit in the heavenly places with Him. My promotion is of the Lord and not from man. I confess boldly that every pit that the enemy has dug for my life will become a stepping stone.

I confess that the prosperity of God rests upon my life. For the Lord makes room for me and increases my capacity. The testimony of the Lord in my life shall be of promotion and operating on a higher dimension. The kind of promotion that will take me from prison to palace comes into my life. I receive divine endorsement.

I believe and confess that the deeper knowledge of the Lord, wisdom from above flows in my life. No temptation shall pull me down, for the Lord Himself promotes me and lifts my hand in the midst of adversity to possess the land.

I confess boldly, that the horn of my strength shall be exalted and the grace of God shall abound in my life for all eyes to see.

I boldly confess that I have come out of sadness into God's joy.

I am blessed and highly favoured.

DIVINE FAVOUR

Genesis 18:3
Genesis 39:21
Exodus 12:36
Judges 21:22
1 Samuel 25:8
Esther 2:17
Job 33:26
Psalm 30:7
Psalm 45:12
Psalm 89:17
Psalm 112:5
Proverbs 11:27
Proverbs 14:9
Proverbs 18:22
Ecclesiastes 9:11
Isaiah 45:1-3
Daniel 1:9
Acts 2:47

Genesis 29:17
Exodus 3:21
Numbers 11:14-15
Ruth 2:13
2 Samuel 15:25
Esther 5:2
Psalm 5:12
Psalm 41:11
Psalm 77:7
Psalm 102:13
Proverbs 3:4
Proverbs 12:2
Proverbs 14:35
Proverbs 22:1
Songs of Solomon 8:10
Isaiah 60:10
Luke 1:28
Acts 7:9-10

Genesis 39:6
Exodus 11:3
Deuteronomy 33:23
1 Samuel 16:22
2 Samuel 20:11
Job 10:12
Psalm 30:5
Psalm 44:3
Psalm 85:1
Psalm 106:4
Proverbs 8:35
Proverbs 13:15
Proverbs 16:15
Proverbs 28:23
Isaiah 26:10
Daniel 1:4
Luke 2:52

1155. Like Elijah pray for the divine ability to overtake those who have gone ahead.

1156. Receive the anointing that will make you disarm satanic kings and take authority.

1157. Thank the Lord in advance for the breakthrough and favour you are expecting.

159

1158. Give God praise for His faithfulness at all time to those who trust in Him.

1159. Thank Him for His plan to prosper you and not to harm you.

1160. Praise the Lord because eye hath not seen nor ear heard what He has in store for you.

1161. Thank the Lord for giving you all things to enjoy in Him.

1162. Pray that you will find the favour for blessing in the sight of the Lord.

1163. Pray that the favour of the Lord will go with you everywhere you are in the name of Jesus.

1164. Pray that the favour of the Lord will manifest even in adverse places like Joseph in the prison.

1165. Pray for the kind of favour God gave Israel to collect the goods of the wicked Egyptians.

1166. Receive the favour of divine elevation in the sight of the enemy.

1167. Pray for the eyes of the Lord to go with you and cause you to stand before Kings.

1168. Pray for the kind of favour Moses found in the sight of the Lord.

1169. Ask the Lord to lead you to those who bless you and not to those who destroy you in the name of Jesus.

1170. Ask the Lord to order your steps to meet those who will believe in the ability of God in you.

1171. Receive the kind of favour that will bring your abilities to the notice of kings.

1172. Thank the Lord for His destined programme

that will bring favour to your life.

1173. Pray for the kind of favour and honour that will frustrate the enemy's plan.

1174. Thank the Lord for the anointing of favour and good understanding which is coming your way.

1175. Pray for the breakthrough idea which will open the door of favour to you.

1176. Ask the Lord to help you develop a craving for His favour more than silver and gold.

1177. Ask the Lord to help you confront the wrong in your children and be favoured with their understanding later.

1178. Pray that you will be patient for the day of your promotion rather than to be in haste.

1179. Give God praise for His kindness which extends to the Heavens.

1180. Confess by faith that you have the life and favour of God in the face of apparent danger.

1181. Pray that the favour of the Lord will be manifest in you everywhere you go, as in the case of Daniel.

1182. Receive the kind of favour which will cause kings to seek after you in the name of Jesus.

1183. Give the Lord praise because He will satisfy you with His favour.

1184. Pray that the blessing of the Lord's favour will make you full of His blessing.

1185. Ask the Lord to surround you with the wall of His favour in the name of Jesus.

1186. In the midst of the weeping that is prolonged, continue to confess that the Lord's favour is forever.

1187. Pray that the Lord will favour you with His divine promotion in the name of Jesus.

1188. Pray for the favour of God's anointing and strength in your life.

1189. Ask the Lord to reveal the favour that brings deliverance in your life.

1190. Pray for the favour of divine wisdom so you can deal wisely in all affairs of life.

1191. Pray that you will flow in favour as you seek to bless other people.

1192. Pray that as you keep serving the Lord, the favour of the Lord will be manifested in all you do.

1193. Confess that the favour of the Lord will not cease in your church.

1194. Pray that the favour of the Lord will rest on your family for generations to come.

1195. Receive the favour which follows a wise servant in the name of the Lord.

1196. Thank the Lord for favour as thick as the cloud of the latter rain which shall rest upon your life.

1197. Pray that the favour of a good spouse will follow you in the name of the Lord.

1198. Ask the Lord to anoint your eyes to see the person of His choosing with whom He has favoured you.

1199. Pray that as the dew upon the grass, the favour of God will rest on your family.

1200. Reflect on your life and thank God for giving you a reason to rejoice.

1201. Like the infant Jesus, pray that the favour of the Lord increases on all that is your own.

1202. Break the wall of resistance between you and people and receive the favour to deal with them.

1203. Give God praise because your appointed time for favour has come.

1204. Give God praise because He will not let the enemy triumph over you.

1205. Thank the Lord for the kind of favour which causes things to flow into your life without sweat.

1206. Bless the name of the Lord because He has given us all things to enjoy in Christ.

1207. Confess that the favour of the Lord will make you a lender not a borrower.

1208. Pray that the favour of God will flow from you to those who are around you.

1209. Praise the Lord for even in a strange land you shall be a carrier of His favour.

1210. Give God praise because His goodness and mercy will follow you all your life.

CONFESSION

I believe and confess that God's plan is to prosper me and not to harm me. God's plan is to elevate me and not to demote me because, eye hath not seen, ear hath not heard nor hath it come into our understanding what God still hath in store for me. For the Lord is giving me joy in all things, causing favour and blessing to flow towards me. The favour of the Lord goes with me everywhere and the Lord's blessing is manifest even in adverse situations. God's favour to collect the goods from the wicked ones rests upon me. God's divine elevation in the sight of the enemy rests upon my life. The eyes of the Lord go with me and cause me to stand before kings and to have favour with all men.

The favour of the Lord brings notice to my life in the presence of those who will bless and promote me God's destined programme will bring favour to my life. I believe and confess that the favour and honour which will frustrate the enemy has rested upon my life. The favour of the Lord which brings me good understanding is coming my way. I am receiving breakthrough ideas which open the doors unto me to help me confront the wrong and be favoured with new understanding. I believe and confess that I will be patient until the day of my promotion.

I confess boldly that the kindness of the Lord upon my life extends to the Heavens. God satisfies my mouth with good things. He took my mourning and gave me laughter, weeping may have been for an night but my joy has come forth. The favour of God's anointing and strength is upon my life, it flows in me and causes me to rise above all situations.

The favour which follows a wise servant is upon my life.

I am blessed and highly favoured.

DIVINE VINDICATION

Genesis 49:19   Deuteronomy 25:1   1 Kings 8:32
2 Chronicles 6:23   Job 11:2   Job 13:18
Psalm 51:4   Psalm 98:1   Isaiah 43:9
Isaiah 50:8   Isaiah 54:17   Matthew 11:19
Matthew 12:37   Titus 3:7   James 2:25
1 John 2:13   Revelation 2:7

1211. Pray that your eyes will see the downfall of the strong enemy that has risen against you.

1212. Pray that you will not be caught unawares by the attack of the enemy.

1213. Nullify every arrow of the enemy which has been targeted at you.

1214. Pray that the Lord will be the watchful eye that executes your vindication.

1215. Ask the Lord to confound the horses and the riders that are against you in the name of the Lord.

1216. Pray for the anointing to triumph and do valiantly in all areas of your life.

1217. Command that those who are pursuing you

unnecessarily end their journey in their own Red Sea.

1218. Command that the oppressor and his weapon will drown in his own Red Sea.

1219. Praise the Lord in advance because He will triumph for you over the enemy.

1220. Ask the Lord to blow the wind of judgement on the camp of those who are pursuing you without cause.

1221. Ask the Lord to accelerate your speed away from the arrow of those who want your soul.

1222. Thank the Lord for putting down every Pharaoh that wants to hold you to shame in the name of Jesus.

1223. Pray that when wronged you will be able to leave it to the Lord and not fight for yourself.

1224. Pray that the victorious work God started in your life will be accomplished in the name of Jesus.

1225. Pray that the Lord will execute the downfall of satan in your life in the name of Jesus.

1226. Confess that every mouth that rises against you in judgement shall be condemned.

1227. Pray that your captivity will be turned around and your impossible situation will turn to a testimony.

1228. Declare that every weapon targeted at your peace will turn around for your blessing.

1229. Give God praise because He always causes us to have victory in the Lord.

1230. Bless the name of the Lord because He will not withhold any good thing from us.

1231. Give God the praise for Jesus who is the captain of our salvation.

1232. Praise the Lord because He knows the counsel of the enemy and shall not be caught unawares.

1233. Pray that the Lord will confound the expectation of the enemy who thinks there is no help for you.

1234. Pray that the Lord will confound the plans of the thousands that may rise against you.

1235. Pray that the Lord will rise and break the cheek bone with which they attack you.

1236. Pray that arm of the Lord will bring victory to your circumstance.

1237. Pray that you will experience the revelation of the arm of the Lord for victory.

1238. Thank the Lord for swallowing up the spirit of death in victory for you.

1239. Pray that your victory which the Lord will bring will not turn into mourning.

1240. Pray that the Lord will bring His victory against your worst enemies in Jesus name.

1241. Pray for the vindication of the Lord which results in the harvest of the blessing of battle.

1242. Receive boldness to take your stand against the wiles of the enemy in the name of Jesus.

1243. Thank the Lord for counting you among the victorious in the name of Jesus.

1244. Receive the faith to overcome the world in the name of Jesus.

1245. Pray that in the face challenges you will always know the victory of the Lord.

1246. Confess that you are coming out of your place of defeat into the victory of the Lord.

1247. Thank the Lord for His promise that they may fight you but they will not overcome you.

1248. Declare the weapon of the enemy ineffective over you in the name of Jesus.

1249. Pray that the victory which the Lord will bring will silence those who hate you.

1250. Thank the Lord for strengthening your hand against your strongest enemies.

1251. Come against every Jericho wall in your way by declaring your victory in Christ.

1252. Nullify the strategies of the Balaks of this world with the blood of Jesus.

1253. Pray that the trap the enemy build will trap him and all of his.

1254. Come against every evil counsel as in the case of Ahithrophel against David.

1255. Ask the Lord to overthrow every Sodom and Gommorrah that stands before your breakthrough.

1256. Thank the Lord for the deliverance you have over sin, for it shall be permanent.

1257. Thank the Lord Jesus for His assurance to us of His victory over the world.

1258. Thank the Lord because through Him we have

overcome the wicked one.

1259. Rejoice because greater is He who is in you than he who is in the world.

1260. Thank the Lord because He will use you to establish His victory in this world.

1261. Confess that because you are born of God you will overcome every challenge that rises against you.

1262. Exercise the faith that overcomes problems by praying and believing for a change.

1263. Thank the Lord because you will taste the fruit of victory in the name of Jesus.

1264. Thank the Lord for the victory you have over death through Christ's death.

1265. Thank the Lord for the victory that brings promotion in the name of Jesus.

1266. Thank the Lord for the victory which puts you above the petty attackers in the name of Jesus.

1267. Thank the Lord for the victory that puts you in the heavenly places of anointing and victory.

1268. Thank the Lord for the victory you have through the blood of Jesus.

1269. Thank the Lord for the victory you have regardless of what you see.

1270. Thank the Lord because Jesus the Lamb has overcome every challenge in advance on your behalf.

1271. Thank the Lord because His divine vindication will cause you to inherit all things in the name of Jesus.

CONFESSION

I believe and confess that the Lord will uphold me at all times, I therefore make progress in all that I do. He shall make the counsel of the enemy be powerless. I believe and confess that the Lord shall confound the expectation of the enemy who say there is no hope for me.

I boldly confess that the Lord rises on my behalf and breaks the cheekbone of the opposition. The Lord Himself will bring victory to my circumstance. I shall experience a revelation of the arm of the Lord; for the Lord Himself shall swallow up the spirit of death and promote victory in my life.

I boldly confess the vindication of the Lord which shall result in my harvest of blessings from all battles. I shall increase on all sides. I boldly take my stand against the wiles of the enemy in the name of Jesus.

By faith I confess that I overcome the world in the name of the Lord. Everything that comes against me one way will flee in seven ways. The weapons of the enemy shall be ineffective over my life. The victory which the Lord brings will silence those who hate me.

Every Jericho wall falls before me for the Lord will strengthen my hand against my strongest enemy. The strategies of the Balaks of this world shall be nullified by the blood of Jesus. The trap of the enemy which was built for me, shall be exposed and destroyed. Every evil counsel of Ahithrophel against me shall not stand. I boldly proclaim my victory and deliverance over sin.

I confess God's assured blessing upon my life. I confess victory over death, victory that brings promotion, victory which puts me above the petty attacks of the enemy, victory that puts me in the heavenly places, victory that applies the blood of Jesus and brings me total vindication.

I am blessed and highly favoured.

DOMINION

Psalm 37:34   Daniel 4:3   Daniel 4:22
Daniel 6:26   Daniel 7:14   Daniel 7:26
Daniel 11:5   1 Peter 4:11

1272. Pray for the anointing to catch up and overtake in the areas of your calling.

1273. Confess that your hand shall be lifted to possess the land.

1274. Like Joseph, pray for the kind of promotion that will take you from prison to palace.

1275. Pray that the Lord who lifts out of the dust will bring His promotion to your life.

1276. Confess the fact that satan and his demons have no dominion over your life in the name of Jesus.

1277. Pray that your actions will be wise and that you will be led of the Lord at all times.

1278. Pray for the boldness and courage to withstand your greatest opposition in the name of the Lord.

1279. Praise the name of the Lord for His victory

and dominion over the challenges of life.

1280. Praise the name of the Lord because He reigns in the affairs of men.

1281. Give God praise because His dominion is an everlasting dominion.

1282. Break the evil dominion of the enemy over your life in the name of Jesus.

1283. Break the hold of presumptuous sin over your life in the name of Jesus.

1284. Exercise your dominion over everything around you in Jesus name.

1285. Confess according to Psalm 49:14 that you shall always have dominion.

1286. Break the attempt of the enemy to put you in bondage through secret sins.

1287. Thank the Lord for the privilege of having everything put under your feet.

1288. Praise the name of the Lord because death no longer has dominion over your life.

1289. Command that everything rising against you remains under your authority in the name of the Lord.

1290. Pray that the Lord will manifest His power against that which proves mightier than you.

1291. Pray that you will reach your destined position as ordained by God.

1292. Pray that the Lord will silence every evil opposition and confound them in the name of Jesus.

1293. Give God praise because dominion and fear

belong to Him and He shall make it known in your life.

1294. Pray that the enemy does not triumph over you in any area of life.

1295. Exercise the authority and dominion which follows the upright in Jesus name.

1296. God exercises dominion from sea to sea; thank Him because that kind of authority goes with you.

1297. Exercise dominion over the challenges that have troubled your mind.

1298. Exercise dominion in the area of your finances in the name of Jesus.

1299. Confess your victory over death regardless of your immediate circumstance.

1300. Thank the Lord for the divine power to loose things on earth and have it granted in heaven.

1301. Exercise authority over every evil attack of satan against your life.

1302. Exercise dominion over every spirit that tries to break the peace of God in your home.

1303. Give God praise because His dominion is an everlasting dominion.

1304. Confess that you disallow sickness and disease in the name of Jesus.

1305. Destroy every generational curse that is hindering your flow in Christ.

1306. Thank the Lord for His command to be fruitful in the land.

1307. Give God praise because everything you do

will be multiplied by the Lord.
1308. Confess that everything around you comes under your subjection.
1309. Give God the praise for the honour of having the whole of creation under you.

CONFESSION

I believe and confess that the Lord is good. I give God praise for His victory and dominion over the challenges of life. I thank the Lord because His dominion is an everlasting dominion.

I boldly confess that God causes me to break the evil dominion of the enemy over my life and to exercise the same dominion over everything around me in the name of Jesus.

According to God's word, I will always have dominion over situations. I command that everything that rises against me will remain under my authority in the name of Jesus. Death has no power over me for the Lord who is mightier is dwell in.

I confess that I will reach my destined position as ordained by the Lord. The enemy will not triumph over any area of my life. I exercise the authority and dominion which follows the upright in Jesus name.

I boldly declare my dominion from place to place. I have dominion over the challenges that have troubled my mind. I have victory over death regardless of my immediate circumstance. I disallow sickness and disease in my body in the name of Jesus. I exercise dominion over every spirit that tries to break the peace of God in my body, in my life and in my home. I thank the Lord for the power to loose on earth all that has been granted by Heaven.

I boldly declare that every generational curse that hinders my flow in Christ is nullified in the name of Jesus and I declare that every spirit contrary to the spirit of Christ is under subjection. For God gives me victory, favour and dominion.

I am blessed and highly favoured.

ENCOURAGEMENT

Deuteronomy 1:38   Deuteronomy 3:28 Judges 20:22
1 Samuel 23:16-17 1 Samuel 30:6   2 Samuel 11:25
2 Chronicles 31:4   2 Chronicles 35:2 Psalm 125:1
Isaiah 41:6-7   1 Corinthians 1:4-7 Colossians 3:16
1 Peter 5:10

1310. Ask the Lord to order your steps to meet those who will believe in the gift of God that is in you.

1311. Receive the kind of favour that will bring your gifts to the notice of kings.

1312. Take authority over the weapons of discouragement and cancel them in the name of Jesus.

1313. Pray that your labour of love will become manifest to those who need encouragement.

1314. Break the hold of discouragement over your spirit in the name of Jesus.

1315. Ask the Lord to use you as a source of encouragement to those who are going through trials.

1316. Thank the Lord for perfecting, establishing and strengthening you at all times.

1317. Take control by encouraging yourself with the Word of God, in the face of adversity.

1318. Confess by faith that whatever you may be facing will turn around for your favour.

1319. Release the power of self-encouragement upon yourself in the name of Jesus.

1320. Worship the Lord with the song of thanksgiving for His faithfulness.

1321. Thank the Lord because He is your portion in every circumstance.

1322. Pray for the strengthening of the Lord in the situation you are facing in the name of the Lord.

1323. Ask the Lord to use you to lift other people's weakened hand in the name of Jesus.

1324. Come against every weapon of discouragement that the enemy is using to attack you.

1325. Thank the Lord because through Him you shall do valiantly for it is He who gives you victory.

1326. Pray for the help of the Lord to come for the situation you are facing.

1327. Confess that according to the Word of God your strength shall be according to your days on earth.

1328. Thank the Lord for the strength and confidence that comes through moments of quietness.

1329. Rejoice in advance as the Lord supplies the strength to face the battles of life.

1330. Ask the Lord to endow you with the kind of

wisdom is which more than strength.

1331. Pray that the Lord will send you help out of Zion and you shall be encouraged.

1332. Pray that your life will be an encouragement to the broken and diseased.

1333. Receive the grace to bring courage and strength to those who have given up.

1334. Confess that the joy of the Lord is your strength in the time of discouragement.

1335. Ask the Lord to send the Jonathans of encouragement in to your life, in Jesus name.

1336. Pray that the counsel of the Lord will come into your life so that your actions will be wise.

1337. Thank the Lord for being your strength, your refuge and your fortress of safety.

1338. Ask the Lord to make haste to your victory in the name of Jesus.

1339. Confess by faith that the hand of the enemy shall not prevail against you in the name of the Lord.

1340. Pray that the Lord will surround you with people who will be a source of encouragement.

1341. Ask the Lord to expose the evil trap of those who want to destroy or discourage you.

1342. Pray that the word that will proceed from you will be that of an encouragement.

1343. Ask the Lord to make you a source of encouragement to those who are weary in the name of Jesus.

1344. Ask the Lord to strengthen you through the entrance of His Word.

1345. Just like David, encourage yourself in the Lord, in the face of betrayal and attack from friends.

1346. Pray that you would draw strength from the Lord in the face of your worst attack.

1347. Receive the grace to overcome the Sanballat and Tobias of discouragement.

1348. Pray that the Lord will turn the place of your previous defeat to the place of victory.

1349. Pray for the grace to encourage the leaders He has placed over you in the name of the Lord.

1350. Ask the Lord to use you to encourage other people to use the gift of God in them.

1351. Pray that the Lord will use you to raise the leaders of the future.

1352. Receive encouragement and strength to overcome the attack of the enemy, in spite of what you are going through.

1353. Ask the Lord to use you to encourage others into the fulfilment of their vision.

1354. Ask the Lord to use you to challenge other people to His service in the name of Jesus.

1355. As iron sharpens iron pray that the blessing of the Lord in your life will encourage others to seek Him.

1356. Come against every trace of selfishness in your life in the name of Jesus.

1357. Receive boldness to discourage evil and promote what glorifies God.

1358. Pray that the entrance of the Word of God in your life will bring encouragement.
1359. Ask for grace to encourage other people in their gift area without jealousy.
1360. Thank the Lord for those saints He uses to challenge you in areas of your Christian life.

CONFESSION

I believe and confess that the Lord is my portion. He has given me the grace to be strengthened in my inner man. I am encouraged, for the Lord is my source. When I am faced with trials or experience betrayal, the presence of the Lord comforts me. The place of my previous defeat has changed to my source of victory.

I confess by faith that God will make me an encouragement to the discouraged. I will be used to lift weak hand. He fills my mouth with encouraging words and uses me to raise other men for His glory. The word of the Lord proceeds from me to encourage other people's vision, calling and blessing.

I believe and confess that I have victory over discouragement, and I have been anointed to overcome the attacks of satan.

I am blessed and highly favoured.

ENDURANCE

Job 14:14
1 Corinthians 4:12
Hebrews 10:32
Hebrews 12:2

Matthew 24:13
2 Corinthians 4:8-9
Hebrews 10:34

Mark 13:13
2 Timothy 2:12
Hebrews 11:27

1361. Thank the Lord because what you are passing through is for a season.
1362. Thank the Lord because He will see you through whatever challenging time you are in.
1363. Pray that you will be strengthened of the Lord not to reward evil for evil.
1364. Thank the Lord for the courage to stand in the face of overwhelming temptations.
1365. Resist everything that wants to stop you from reaching your goal in Jesus name.
1366. Give God the praise for His faithfulness in your life at all times.
1367. Thank Him for seeing you through major and minor challenges of life.
1368. Pray for the grace to overcome every battle to

the end in the name of Jesus.

1369. Take authority over every attack of discouragement in the name of Jesus.

1370. Pray that you will endure every persecution of the enemy in the name of the Lord.

1371. Take authority over every lie of satan perpetrated against you and declare that they shall have no effect in the name of the Lord.

1372. Ask the Lord to help you not to let what you are going through stop you from where you are going.

1373. Declare your freedom from the attitude of despair and receive boldness from the Lord.

1374. Thank the Lord because He has promised to be with you and not forsake you.

1375. Pray for the grace to keep your eyes on the Lord in the face of the challenges of life.

1376. Ask for the grace to follow Him to the end no matter what you go through.

1377. Release yourself to the Holy Spirit and ask Him to open your eyes to the steps to take in every situation in the name of Jesus.

1378. Receive the grace to manifest the fruit of patience in all circumstances.

1379. Pray that you will endure like Moses did, in the face of the temptation to compromise.

1380. Ask for the grace to have your eyes constantly on the Lord and not the circumstance.

1381. Confess by faith that even the attacks of the devil on your life and property will turn around for your good.

1382. Thank the Lord because He will strengthen you to endure until you obtain the promise.

1383. Confess boldly in the face of a prolonged challenge that you will wait until change come.

1384. Confess that you shall endure all things until salvation comes.

1385. Declare by faith that every attempt of satan to quench the light of God in you shall become null and void.

1386. Pray that your eyes will constantly be on Jesus the author and finisher of your faith.

1387. The Lord Jesus endured the cross by despising its shame, ask for grace from the Lord to overcome totally in all areas.

CONFESSION

I believe and confess that the Lord is good. His faithfulness abounds for me at all times. God is my source of encouragement in the I face of major and minor problems. What I am going through shall not stop me from where He is taking me. I am free from despair and fear. My eyes are on the Lord and He shall see me through to the end of the matter.

I boldly confess that my steps are ordered of the Lord and He shall lead me to the path of success.

The Lord gives me the fruit of patience, and no weapon of satan shall quench the light of God in me.

My eyes are on the Lord the Author and Finisher of my faith. I shall endure until the promise becomes a reality.

I am blessed and highly favoured.

EXAMPLE

Matthew 20:26-28   **John 13:15**   **Romans 10:17**
1 Corinthians 10:6   **2 Corinthians 3:18**   **1 Timothy 4:12**
James 5:10   **1 Peter 2:21**

1388. Ask the Lord to help you to shine as light in this crooked world.

1389. Receive freedom from the bondage of gossip and other sins of the mouth.

1390. Ask the Lord to cleanse your heart from every trace of dirty thoughts.

1391. Thank the Lord for those whom He has used as examples to challenge you in your Christian life.

1392. Thank the Lord for those who spent time to build you in the things of God.

1393. Give God praise for the strength and faithfulness of the Lord has upheld you.

1394. Thank the Lord for those whom He is bringing around you for you to be an example to.

1395. Pray that your life will be a testimony to the glory of the Lord.

1396. Ask the Lord to give the spirit of a servant, to serve others like Jesus did.

1397. Pray that when people look at your life they will see the glory and righteousness of the Lord.

1398. Pray that other people's life will be better by observing your life.

1399. Ask the Lord to use the words of your mouth to build others.

1400. Ask the Lord to help you so that the words that proceed from your mouth will be faith building.

1401. Pray that your life will manifest the transformation that the Holy Spirit brings.

1402. Ask for the grace to yield to the Holy Spirit so that your life will always be a challenge to those around you.

1403. Pray that the Lord would remove whatever will make others stumble as they observe your life.

1404. Receive the grace to be an example to believers in all areas of life, in the name of Jesus.

1405. Ask for the grace to walk as an example in the face of the worst provocation.

1406. Pray that when wronged you will be able to leave it to the Lord and not fight for yourself.

1407. Thank the Lord for the privilege to be counted

worthy to experience persecution for being a believer.

1408. Ask the Lord for the grace to an able witness for the Lord Jesus Christ, who loved you and gave His life for you.

1409. Pray for the grace to walk and live even as Christ lived during His earthly life.

1410. Ask the Lord to help you so that those who observe your life will not stumble but stand for the Lord.

CONFESSION

I believe and confess that the Lord is good. His faithfulness is forever. The Lord has called me to be a testimony of His power. He has endued me with the spirit of a servant to serve like Jesus did. My life shall be a challenge to those who observe. The words that proceed from me will build other people.

I boldly confess that I am an example of God's blessing, favour and goodness. I manifest the transformation which the Holy Spirit achieves.

By faith I receive the grace to overcome persecution and refuse to take vengeance and be an able witness of Jesus Christ.

I am blessed and highly favoured.

FAITH

Proverbs 20:6   Proverbs 28:20   Matthew 9:29
Matthew 17:20   Romans 10:17   Romans 12:3
2 Corinthians 5:7   Galatians 3:11   Hebrews 2:4
Hebrews 11:3   Hebrews 11:39   Hebrews 10:23
1 Peter 1:7   1 Peter 5:9   1 John 5:4
Jude 3   Jude 20

1411. Pray that you will find your true self-worth in Christ at all times in Jesus name.

1412. Shout unto God with the voice of triumph in the face of every challenge.

1413. Bind the spirit of fear from controlling your life in the name of the Lord.

1414. Thank the Lord for causing you to have victory through the Lord Jesus Christ.

1415. Give God praise for helping you to grow from faith to faith.

1416. Pray that you will always move and operate on the basis of faith and not sight.

1417. Ask the Lord to help you to stay in the word of God so that your faith can grow.

1418. Speak a change to the mountain of challenges in your life.

1419. Command the mountains of life you are facing to bow to the word of God.

1420. Begin to declare by faith that the things you hope for will come to pass.

1421. No matter what contradictory circumstance you are facing, confess that the word of God will work for you.

1422. Take authority over the situation which satan is magnifying in the natural and declare your victory in the name of Jesus.

1423. Begin to confess what the word of God says concerning the challenges of life and not what satan says.

1424. Confess what the word of God says you are and not what satan says.

1425. Fear is the opposite of faith, take authority over it and break its hold over your life.

1426. Declare by faith that you will always be led by the word and not the traditions of men.

1427. Thank God for the privilege of knowing Christ and confess that you will enjoy the privileges in the name of the Lord.

1428. Confess by faith that satan and his demons have no dominion over your life in the name of Jesus.

1429. Pray that your faith will produce financial, spiritual and emotional prosperity in your life.

1430. Pray for the grace to overcome the things that may be hindering your faith.

1431. Pray that the entrance of God's word into your life will produce growth and maturity.

1432. Pray that the kind of faith by which God spoke the universe into existence will operate in you.

1433. Ask the Lord to help you to only take actions that correspond with faith.

1434. Ask the Lord to help you so you can hold on to your confession of faith.

1435. Make a vow to the Lord that as a child of God you will live by faith.

1436. Gain control by encouraging yourself with the word of God in the face of adversity.

1437. Pray for the grace to operate in the faith that leads to commitment.

1438. Confess by faith that you will enjoy the blessings of a faithful man.

1439. Thank the Lord for filling you with the kind of faith that overcomes the world.

1440. Earnestly stand against everything that does not affirm your walk of faith.

1441. Pray that your faith will grow and increase in the capacity to deliver.

1442. Pray that every trial you face will result in the strengthening of your faith.

1443. Exercise your faith by using it to resist the devil right now in the name of Jesus.

1444. Like the saints of old subdue every manifestation of the kingdom of satan.

1445. Confess by faith that you obtain a good report

through the exercise of your faith.
1446. Begin to speak your desire, believing that it
shall come to pass.

CONFESSION

I thank the Lord for causing me to have victory through the Lord Jesus Christ.

I boldly declare that I am filled with the God kind of faith. The faith of God in me strengthens me to speak to the mountains of challenges. The mountains bow to the Word of God. My hope comes to pass. My vision is realised.

By faith I come against situations and circumstances and gain control through the Lord Jesus Christ. Fear is not my portion. Traditions of man shall not control me. Satan and his demons have no control over me. I am filled with the faith that overcomes the world.

Through faith I speak to every satanic manifestation and produce financial and spiritual prosperity.

By faith I confess that I shall enjoy the blessings of a faithful man and obtain a good report through the exercise of my faith.

I am blessed and highly favoured.

FAITHFULNESS OF GOD

Psalm 36:5   Psalm 40:10   Psalm 89:1-2
Psalm 89:5   Psalm 89:8   Psalm 89:24
Psalm 89:33   Psalm 92:2   Psalm 119:90
Isaiah 25:1   Lamentation 3:22-23 Revelation 2:10

1447. Thank the Lord for the accelerated breakthrough that will make you recover wasted years.

1448. Give God the praise for His faithfulness at all times in your life.

1449. Praise the Lord because He began a good work in you and He will finish it in the name of Jesus.

1450. Praise the Lord because His faithfulness is as high as the heavens.

1451. Declare the faithfulness of God even as you face the challenges of Life.

1452. Pray that God's faithfulness will be your experience on a day-by-day basis.

1453. Ask for the counsel and the guidance of the Lord as you face major and minor decisions of life.

1454. Thank the Lord because His faithfulness will never fail.

1455. Praise the name of the Lord because He is a covenant keeping God.

1456. Pray that the Lord will lead you continually and that you will not miss His plan.

1457. Ask the Lord for His guidance in the midst of the darkness of this world.

1458. Pray that you will experience the faithfulness of God and to know His tender mercies.

1459. Receive grace to do the will of God at all times in the name of the Lord.

1460. Thank God because He started a good work in you and He will finish it in the name of the Lord.

1461. Give God the praise because He will always be sufficient for you.

1462. Pray for the grace to trust the Lord with unwavering trust in Him.

1463. Commit your vision to the Lord and confess your absolute trust in Him.

1464. Rejoice because of the knowledge that God will never lie, but He will keep His promises.

1465. Thank God because He will be with you even unto the ends of the earth.

1466. Pray that His loving kindness and mercy will preserve you in the presence of the enemy.

1467. Pray that every attempt of the enemy to belittle the goodness of God will be negated by the blood of Jesus.

CONFESSION

I believe and confess that the Lord is good. I thank the Lord for His faithfulness at all times in my life. The faithfulness of the Lord is known to me as I face the challenges of life. God will not fail me for He is a covenant keeping God.

His faithfulness makes guidance available in the darkness of this world. His faithfulness will make Him finish what He started in my life. The Lord is more than enough for me, and I trust Him even on to the ends of the earth.

I am blessed and highly favoured.

FAMILY

Genesis 18:19   Genesis 47:12   Deuteronomy 12:7
Deuteronomy 14:26 Deuteronomy 15:20 Deuteronomy 33:11
Proverbs 20:7   Psalm 68:6   Psalm 113:9
Matthew 10:36   Luke 19:9   Acts 16:31
Acts 18:8   1 Corinthians 16:19 Galatians 6:10
Ephesians 2:19   Ephesians 3:15   1 Timothy 3:4-5
1 Timothy 3:12   1 Timothy 3:15   1 Timothy 5:14
2 Timothy 1:16   2 Timothy 4:19   Hebrews 3:4-5

1468. Pray that the Lord will show you loopholes in your own family life that can hurt you.

1469. Exercise dominion over every spirit that tries to break the peace of God in your home.

1470. Ask the Lord to bring a godly satisfaction into your marriage in the name of Jesus.

1471. Break the impact of the curse of sexual impurity in the name of Jesus.

1472. Break the power of the curse of incest over your life in the name of Jesus.

1473. Repent and break the hold of the curse of bestiality in your life and family.

1474. Pray that God will give you the kind of favour

which will make your children rise and call you blessed.

1475. Prophecy into the future of your children that they will manifest God's blessing.

1476. Speak the blessing of the Lord on all your children and the future generation.

1477. Break the hold of every evil pronouncement made into your life in the past in Jesus name.

1478. Cancel every seed that the enemy may have planted in your life through previous sexual entanglements.

1479. Give God the praise for His faithfulness in providing for your family.

1480. Pray that God will fill your heart with pure love for the members of your household.

1481. Pray that the Lord will fill your heart with love for your spouse even in times of differences.

1482. Pray for the barren women you know that they will become joyful mothers of children.

1483. Pray for a continuous flow of joy in your marriage relationship.

1484. Pray that the subsequent years of your marriage will bring blessing and glory to God.

1485. Possess the future for your children by prophesying blessing into their future.

1486. Ask the Lord to heal your marriage from the impact of selfish behaviours.

1487. Receive healing for any heavy handed way your parent dealt with you in the past.

1488. Destroy the impact of ungodly competit
between you and your spouse in the name
Jesus.

1489. Break the negative impact which been spoilt as a
child and been allowed to have your way has
had on you.

1490. As the scripture states, pray that you will
approach marriage as a subject of honour.

1491. Pray for the grace to face the challenge and be
committed to your marriage.

1492. Pray for the wisdom to submit to your spouse
even in the times of differences of views.

1493. Thank the Lord for what He is doing in your
family in the name of Jesus.

1494. Give God the praise because He is a covenant
keeping God.

1495. Pray that the spirit of companionship will
prevail in your marriage.

1496. Thank God for making His love to be manifest
in your marriage.

1497. Come against every vow you may have made
that is causing problem in your marriage.

1498. Ask the Lord to make you and your spouse
one in your marriage.

1499. Ask the Lord to deliver you from the
emotional baggage you inherited from your
parents.

1500. Pray the Holy Spirit will always open your
eyes to the good qualities in your spouse.

1501. Pray that the blessing God has given your

family will not cause division.

1502. Take authority over every financial mountain facing your family and receive breakthrough.

1503. Pray for your teenage children that they will boldly say no to ungodly influence.

1504. Stand against the negative influence of all third parties in the name of Jesus.

1505. Pray for the wisdom to raise your children with love and not rules.

1506. Bind the spirit of strife from encroaching into your family in Jesus name.

1507. Bind the spirit of jealousy from operating in your marriage, and release the love of God.

1508. Ask the Lord for the strength to overcome the temptation of ridiculing your spouse.

1509. Resist every anti-marriage demon released to operate against your home.

1510. Pray for your teens that they will not succumb to the trap of immorality in the name of Jesus.

1511. Draw a blood-line against the spirit of divorce in your home.

1512. Thank the Lord for His continuous supply of finance to your family.

1513. Pray that the love that now binds you and your spouse will be even stronger.

1514. Pray as a parent that you will not be over-possessive or over-permissive.

1515. Thank the Lord for the wonderful family He has given you according to His promise.

1516. Pray for the grace to be submissive to your

husband according to the word of God.

1517. Pray that communication in your marriage will be regular, strong and positive.

1518. Pray that God's divine order will take over in your marriage.

1519. Ask the Lord to help you make your home a light in the darkness of these world.

1520. Reject every negative world pronounced into your children at school or other places.

1521. Confess that your children will be head and not tail and builders of God's kingdom.

1522. Speak into the future of your children, that they will be fulfilled in their marriage.

1523. Thank the Lord because He began a good work in your marriage and He will complete it.

1524. Pray that you will truly be a good example of our heavenly father.

1525. Pray that when family look at you they will be drawn to God.

1526. Pray that your home will be filled with unconditional love.

1527. Ask the Lord to help you not to drain but fill your children up emotionally.

1528. Come against the critical spirit that is tearing your home apart in the name of the Lord.

CONFESSION

I believe and confess that God is good. I thank the Lord for His faithfulness in my family. I receive the grace of God to maintain unity and love in my marriage.

No weapon formed against my home shall stand, and every mouth that rises against me in judgement, shall be condemned. Every demon against marriage is commanded to leave my home. The spirit of jealousy is bound from coming near my home. My children are covered with the blood of Jesus. My home shall be a place of divine order.

I give God glory because He began a good work in my home and He shall complete it.

I am blessed and highly favoured.

FEAR

Exodus 15:16   Proverbs 4:23   Isaiah 54:14
Matthew 10:28   Matthew 17:7   Mark 5:36
Mark 6:50   Philippians 1:14   Hebrews 13:6
1 John 4:18   Revelation 1:17

1529. Take authority over everything that constitutes *"lions and snakes"* and subdue them in Jesus name.
1530. Boldly confess that you shall not be held in bondage to the spirit of fear.
1531. Cancel the curse of restlessness and the bondage of fear in your life.
1532. Pray for the power to withstand the evil gates of the enemy in the name of Jesus.
1533. Ask the Lord to help you protect your heart diligently from that which is not profitable.
1534. Come against every spirit of fear and confusion of mind in the name of the Lord.
1535. Break yourself free from the fear of an economic downturn in the future.

1536. Thank the Lord for giving you victory over the challenges of life.

1537. Thank Him because He has promised not to leave you nor forsake you.

1538. Thank the Lord for the boldness to face the challenges of the daily Christian life.

1539. Praise Him because according to Him, the weapons of the enemy shall not overcome you.

1540. Declare to yourself that you have not received the spirit of fear, but that of boldness and a sound mind.

1541. Break the hold of the spirit of fear over your future in the name of the Lord.

1542. Ask the Lord to fill you with a holy fear of Him and not the fear of the enemy.

1543. Ask the Lord to fill you with His Holy dread in the name of Jesus.

1544. Command that your dread will be in the heart of those who have risen against you in the name of Jesus.

1545. Confess that you will dwell safely and nothing shall make you afraid in the name of the Lord.

1546. Pray that the Lord will fill you with a heart that truly reverence Him.

1547. Take authority over the things that have filled you with worry and fear in the name of Jesus.

1548. Pray that in the midst of the things that have troubled your mind you will hear the voice of the Lord clearly.

1549. Rejoice by faith in anticipation of God turning news contrary to your joy around.

1550. Ask the Lord to open your eyes to the secret of worry free living in the name of Jesus.

1551. Break the hold of fear over the people of your household.

1552. Receive boldness to preach the word of God without the fear of men.

1553. Commit your future into God's hand ask for the grace to trust Him without doubting.

1554. Break every tormenting effect which fear has had on your life and receive freedom.

1555. Ask the Lord to deliver you from unnecessary suspicion and fear in your relationships.

1556. Confess boldly that because the Lord is your strength, you refuse to be afraid of any man.

1557. Take authority over the spirit of fear and oppression and declare that they shall be far from you.

1558. Pray that your fear and dread will fall on those who have risen against you.

1559. Thank the Lord for filling your heart with a godly fear.

CONFESSION

I believe and confess that I have victory over the challenges of life, for the Lord has promised not to leave or forsake me. I receive boldness instead of fear to face the challenges.

I boldly declare that the weapons of the enemy shall have no effect on me. I reject the interference of the spirit of fear. The fear of the future, failure, the fear of success, and all other fears. I break every tormenting effect which fear has had over my life, and I declare that all news contrary to my joy shall be turned around. I receive the heart of a Godly fear to honour and magnify the Lord, and not the problems. I receive God's grace to trust Him without doubt.

I am blessed and highly favoured.

FINANCE

Deuteronomy 8:18
1 Kings 17:15-16
Psalm 50:14
Isaiah 48:17
Proverbs 10:4
Malachi 3:10
Mark 11:23-25
Luke 12:31-32
1 Corinthians 9:7-10
Ephesians 4:28
3 John 2

Deuteronomy 28:1-6
Psalm 23:5
Psalm 78:14
Proverbs 3:9-10
Proverbs 10:22
Matthew 6:33
Luke 5:6-7
Luke 12:42-44
2 Corinthians 9:7
Ephesians 5:1

Joshua 1:8
Psalm 35:27
Isaiah 1:19
Proverbs 8:12
Proverbs 24:3-4
Matthew 25:22-23
Luke 6:38
Luke 16:11
Ephesians 3:20
James 4:3

1560. Thank the Lord because He will make you a lender and not a borrower.

1561. Pray that you will be a lender and not a borrower in Jesus name.

1562. Break the cycle of poverty and confess that your soul shall be satisfied.

1563. Confess that the favour of the Lord will make you a lender not a borrower.

1564. Reverse the curse pronounced against your source of income.

1565. Destroy the effect of every economic and

financial dealing that is false in the name of Jesus.

1566. Repent of the spirit of materialism which has manifested itself in those who have withheld what they should give to God.

1567. Sever every control of the spirit of poverty over your life in the name of the Lord.

1568. Give God the praise for His faithfulness in providing for your family.

1569. Confess that the quicksand of debt will not swallow you in the name of the Lord.

1570. Pray that you will be used of God to sponsor the things of the kingdom.

1571. Ask the Lord to help you to be a channel for meeting the needs of your family.

1572. Break the yoke of poverty over your family in the name of Jesus.

1573. Thank the Lord because He will use you to establish His kingdom.

1574. Pray that the Lord will provide the means for the supply of your material need.

1575. Receive by faith the blessing that makes rich in the name of Jesus.

1576. Pray that you will always have the seed of finance to minister to other people.

1577. Pray that you will be a blessing to those who lack.

1578. Pray that your wealth will be used to reach people for Christ.

1579. Ask the Holy Spirit to give you a heart that is

obedient.

1580. Pray that the blessing which follows the obedient will follow you in the name of Jesus.

1581. Pray that the seed of your investment into the things of the kingdom will bring forth fruit in Jesus name.

1582. Pray that the Lord will move you from seed-time to bumper harvest time in the name of Jesus.

1583. Prophesy increase and growth to your seed in the name of the Lord.

1584. Ask the Holy Spirit to make your heart tender in sowing towards the harvest.

1585. Pray that the business of the kingdom will be of priority in your life in the name of Jesus.

1586. Confess that your receiving will increase in the name of the Lord.

1587. Break the hold of the spirit of selfishness over your life in the name of Jesus.

1588. Confess that the chambers of your life will be filled with His abundant riches.

1589. Confess that the blessing which follows obedience will follow your life.

1590. Receive by faith the favour which comes through giving.

1591. Pray that you will always be covered by the favour of the Lord.

1592. Vow to the Lord that as He blesses you, you will be used to fund the end-time gospel.

1593. Receive the power to create wealth in the

name of Jesus.

1594. Worship the Lord who is your father and He owns the cattle on a thousand hills.

1595. Confess by faith that you will partake of the wealth of the wicked being transferred to the believers.

1596. Confess by faith that your labour shall not be in vain.

1597. Thank the Lord in advance for physical and financial promotion.

1598. Pray for the anointing of faithfulness to the service of financial stewardship.

1599. Confess that as a servant of the Lord you will prosper and go forward.

1600. Thank the Lord for His plan for your prosperity.

1601. Prophesy great measures of favour and increase into your life.

1602. Prophesy the kind of blessing which there is no room to receive.

1603. Praise the Lord for His prosperous kingdom that is coming into your life.

1604. Praise the Lord for adding freely to your life that which the ungodly crave.

1605. Reach forth and claim the marvellous blessings God has earmarked for you.

1606. Proclaim in the presence of your greatest challenge that you possess the power to get wealth.

1607. Receive the anointing that will lead to creative

ideas in the name of Jesus.

1608. Ask the Lord to open your eyes to that which shall be profitable.

1609. Pray that the Lord will deliver you from time wasting ventures.

1610. Thank the Lord for the promise He made to give you good success.

1611. Pray for the heart that follows the path of the obedience and leads to promotion.

1612. God is a giver, ask for the attitude of a giver like God.

1613. Prophesy that the barrel of God's supply to your life shall not dry up in your life.

1614. Thank the Lord because the windows of heaven are opened on your life.

1615. Receive grace from the Lord to fulfil the vows you have made.

1616. Prophesy an overflowing blessing into your life in the name of Jesus.

1617. Pray for the kind of turn around of blessing that fills an empty net to breaking point.

1618. Pray that the Lord will move in your life beyond your wildest imagination.

1619. Thank the Lord for making you to be above only and not under.

1620. Pray that the increase of wealth will not affect your commitment to the Lord.

1621. Thank the Lord for loading you with enough and leftover to bless others.

1622. Pray that your going in and out will carry the

favour and blessing of the Lord.

1623. Give the Lord praise because your day of overflowing blessing is here.

1624. Repent of all the times you put limitation on God in your words and deeds.

1625. Ask the Lord to bless the work of your hand and cause it to increase.

1626. Rejoice for the understanding that your increase and blessing pleasures God.

1627. Thank the Lord because what He is doing your life will not be accompanied by sorrow.

1628. Ask for the grace to be a faithful steward in all that you do.

1629. Pray for grace to be diligent and faithful in your employment.

1630. Confess God's protection over all that the Lord has blessed you with.

1631. Praise the Lord for the promotion which places you above everything.

1632. Give God praise because your hands have been blessed of Him to produce wealth.

1633. Ask the Lord for a heart that obeys Him in giving.

1634. Take authority over every kind of devourer the enemy is using against your finances.

1635. Pray that the Lord will expose any unforgiveness that can hinder your blessing.

1636. Pray that God's promise of breakthrough will be a reality in your life.

1637. Ask the Lord for a heart that will use God's

blessing the right way.

1638. Command that every treasure which belongs to you and has been stolen by the enemy will begin to come your way.

CONFESSION

I believe and confess that the Lord is good. He is faithful to all those who trust in Him.

I give God praise for His increase in my life and the blessing which He has brought. I rejoice because the Lord has brought to my life the blessing that makes rich. He has given me the seed of finance to minister to others, who lack. This is my day of harvest. This is my time of increasing in everything I do. The storehouse is full with God's abundance.

Through God I declare my freedom from the shackles of debt. I worship the Lord who owns the cattle upon a thousand hills. We give Him praise for making me a partaker of the wealth of the wicked. I am financially buoyant in Christ, enjoying His increase everyday.

I am blessed and highly favoured.

Focus

Joshua 1:5-8   Psalm 112:7   Isaiah 50:7
Luke 9:62   2 Corinthians 4:18   Philippians 3:14
Philippians 4:8   Hebrews 12:2

1639. Receive the grace to focus on the mark of your calling.

1640. Confess that by faith you will rise to your destined calling in the name of the Lord.

1641. Give God praise for the wondrous works He is doing in your life daily.

1642. Thank the Lord for the benefits of salvation, which you enjoy in Christ.

1643. Take authority over every time consuming distraction of satan and break free from it.

1644. Pray for a steady focus on your calling and goals in Christ.

1645. Confess by faith that since your hand is on the tool of service, you will not look back.

1646. Pray that the work and programme of God's kingdom will be your priority.

1647. Reject and refuse every programme, vision and task that is not God's calling for your life.

1648. Pray for deliverance from every time wasting dream that is not God's original intention for you.

1649. Receive the anointing to pursue and achieve the calling of God for your life.

1650. Confess that you will make it to the prize of the high calling of God for your life.

1651. Take authority over every tendency of jealousy over other people's gifts in Jesus name.

1652. Ask the Lord to open your eyes to the gifting He has deposited in you.

1653. Pray that you will flow and maximise the gift of God in you.

1654. Take authority over every form of confusion of mind and pray for the ability to stay focused.

1655. Receive the grace to be comfortable in the presence of other gifted people.

1656. Pray that you will become a meaningful specific in the area of your calling.

1657. Ask for the grace to keep your eye on the breakthrough coming despite contrary reports.

1658. Ask the Lord to help you so that your focus will be determined by the word of God.

1659. Break the control of that which takes your attention off the word of God.

1660. Confess by faith that the roaring of the enemy like a lion will not stop your victory in Jesus name.

1661. Thank the Lord because you shall possess your possession and see your vision fulfilled.

1662. Reject every association that draws you away from your focus in the name of the Lord.

1663. Break the influence of every negative friendships and associations in the name of Jesus.

1664. Pray that the Lord will open your eyes to the true intentions of those seeking your attention.

1665. Destroy the yoke of the evil habits that are holding you and clouding your vision.

1666. Ask the Lord for the grace to stay away from the associations that are not helping your spiritual progress.

1667. Pray that the Lord will bring vision-building friends into your life.

1668. Pray for the ability to focus on life building virtues in the name of Jesus.

1669. Pray that as you started the journey of faith you will not stop until you finish well.

1670. Just as God directed Elijah to the brook and the widow, ask Him to direct your step in life.

1671. Receive grace from the Lord to loose yourself from every excess weight of negative relationships.

1672. Pray that your heart will always be filled and guided by the Holy Spirit.

CONFESSION

I give God praise for the wondrous work He is doing in my life. I thank God because He is the Author and Finisher of my faith.

I boldly reject every form of satanic destruction and break free from them. My life is anointed to carry out the programme of God. Therefore, I reject every time wasting dream, and every tendency of jealousy over other people's gifts.

The grace of the Lord abounds on to me and opens me to the giftings deposited in me. I shall possess my possession and see the fulfilment of my vision. My eyes are on the breakthrough despite contrary report. I break free from ungodly habits that are holding me back.

I am blessed and highly favoured.

FORGIVENESS

Numbers 14:18	Deuteronomy 21:8	Psalm 25:18
Psalm 32:1	Psalm 32:5	Psalm 78:38
Psalm 99:8	Jeremiah 31:34	Amos 7:2
Matthew 6:12	Matthew 6:14	Mark 2:5
Mark 11:25	Luke 7:43	Luke 7:48
Luke 11:4	Romans 4:7	Romans 12:14
2 Corinthians 2:10	Ephesians 1:7	Ephesians 4:32
Colossians 1:14	Colossians 2:13	Colossians 3:13
James 5:15	1 John 1:9	1 John 2:12

1673. Thank the Lord for His forgiveness that flows to us because God is full of compassion.

1674. Ask the Lord for the heart that is moved with compassion towards others.

1675. Praise the Lord for His promise that He shall not retain His anger forever.

1676. Pray that you will be surrounded by His mercy and compassion at all times.

1677. Take the time to give God the praise for who He is and what He is doing in your life.

1678. Thank Him for His mercy that endures forever.

1679. Thank the Lord for taking care of your past and guaranteeing your future.

1680. Thank the Lord for the forgiveness of your sin and cleansing you from unrighteousness.

1681. Ask the Lord to give you a heart that is tender to forgive others.

1682. Pray for the heart that truly receives forgiveness from others in the name of the Lord.

1683. Release those who have offended you in the past so that they do not hinder your prayer.

1684. Ask the Lord for the grace to make the first move even where you feel violated.

1685. Thank the Lord for His compassion and forgiveness of all your sins.

1686. Ask the Lord to look upon your life with His compassion and forgive you.

1687. Thank the Lord for His promise to forgive and not remember your sins any more.

1688. Thank the Lord with a grateful heart for the forgiveness of your sins.

1689. Ask the Lord to help you to grow a heart that forgives and forbears for one another.

1690. Give God the praise for being the God who forgives iniquities and transgression.

1691. Plead the blood of Jesus against the hold of an unforgiving spirit over your life in the name of Jesus.

1692. Thank the Lord because He is faithful and just to forgive all sins.

1693. Receive the grace to give forgiveness to those

who have offended you in the name of Jesus.

1694. Ask the Lord for a heart that is tender and that gives forgiveness in the name of Jesus.

1695. Ask the Lord to help you to exercise unconditional love like God gave you.

1696. Pray that the Holy Spirit will rid you of the offences you have held against people.

1697. Ask the Lord to heal you from all the pains that may have been inflicted on you which makes it hard to forgive.

1698. Ask the Lord for the ability to bless and not curse those who have offended you.

1699. Repent of any tendency to wish evil on those who have offended you.

1700. Receive from the Lord the ability to live peaceably with all men.

1701. Thank the Lord for the riches of His grace that brought you salvation.

1702. Thank the Lord for the redeeming power of His blood.

1703. Receive the grace to be clothed with love in all your relationships.

1704. Thank the Lord for redeeming your life from destruction and setting your feet on solid rock.

1705. Destroy every curse which previous stand of unforgiveness may have brought on you.

CONFESSION

I believe and confess that the Lord is good and His mercy endures forever. The Lord has changed my mourning into dancing again, for He has cleansed me from all unrighteousness and sin.

I believe and confess that the riches of God's grace abound on to me and helps me to forgive those who have offended me.

God fills me with unconditional love so I refuse to live in offence against other people. I choose to bless and not to curse. I choose to wish good to people and not evil. I have found that I have the ability to live in peace, for I am filled with the love of God. The Lord has redeemed my life from destruction and set my feet on the solid Rock.

I am blessed and highly favoured.

FREEDOM FROM BONDAGE

Genesis 45:7	Leviticus 26	Numbers 31:5
Deuteronomy 27:16-26	Deuteronomy 28	Judges 3:9
Judges 15:18	2 Samuel 22:2	2 Kings 5:1
2 kings 13:17	1 Chronicles 4:10	1 Chronicles 11:14
2 Chronicles 12:7	Ezra 9:13	Esther 4:14
Psalm 18:50	Psalm 22:4	Psalm 32:7
Psalm 44:4	Psalm 70:5	Psalm 144:2
Proverbs 11:8-9	Proverbs 11:21	Proverbs 28:26
Isaiah 49:24-25	Joel 2:32	Obadiah 17
Matthew 11:28	Luke 4:18	Romans 11:26

1706. Break the attempt of the enemy to put you in bondage through secret sins.

1707. Break the cycle of poverty and lack that has been in your family from generations.

1708. Break the curse of oppression and bondage from your family in the name of the Lord.

1709. Break the bondage of servitude to those who hate you.

1710. Confess that you choose to walk in the blessing of the Lord and reject every curse.

1711. Break every barrier that is holding you from

entering a new realm of blessing.

1712. Prophecy change to every prevailing circumstance you are facing.

1713. Destroy the yoke which people have placed on your life.

1714. Ask the Lord to deliver you from the emotional baggage you inherited from your parents.

1715. Break the curse of worshipping any ungodly image in your family.

1716. Break the curse of disrespect for your family militating against your family.

1717. Break the curse of offence which you committed against your neighbour dating back to generations.

1718. Break the curse, which comes as a result of misleading the disabled.

1719. Break the curse, which comes as a result of offence against an alien.

1720. Break the impact of the curse of incest in your family in the name of Jesus.

1721. Break the curse of participating in sexual sin in Jesus name.

1722. Break the curse, which comes as a result of bestiality.

1723. Break the curse, which comes with committing sin with your in-laws.

1724. Break the power of the curse, which comes as a result of managing your neighbours behind them.

1725. Break the generational come which follows

destroying the innocent.

1726. Break the curse, which follows disobedience to the word of God.

1727. Break the curse, which may have come on your business and your income.

1728. Ask the Lord to silence the enemy and the avenger in your life in Jesus name.

1729. Pray that the Lord will crush every lie of satan under your feet shortly.

1730. Cast down imagination and anything that says you do not have your desired result.

1731. Destroy every curse which your previous stand of unforgiveness may have brought on you.

1732. Bind every spirit of confusion that may want to attack you.

1733. Pray that the hurts of the past will not hinder the flow of your joy in the future.

1734. Receive freedom from the tendency to be abusive in the name of Jesus.

1735. Pray that you will be tender and be free from an aggressive spirit.

1736. Ask the Lord to help you overcome the constant feeling of dissatisfaction.

1737. Receive freedom from the bondage of gossip and other sins of the mouth.

1738. Ask the Lord to cleanse your heart from every trace of dirty thoughts.

1739. Receive deliverance from the bondage of depression in the name of the Lord.

1740. Thank the Lord for setting you free from

tendencies of a desperate spirit.

1741. Ask the Holy Spirit to rid your heart of a fault-finding spirit.

1742. Receive freedom from a defeatist spirit and walk in boldness.

1743. Break yourself free from a critical and fault-finding spirit.

1744. Ask the Lord to help you overcome the tendency to be arrogant.

1745. Receive the cleansing of the Holy Spirit for every problem of cursing and swearing.

1746. Humble yourself before the Lord and be free from every hold of egotism.

1747. Humble yourself before the Lord and be free from every hold of arrogance.

1748. Confess that you are free from a doubtful spirit and now full of faith.

1749. Pray that you will be free from an unhealthy competitive spirit in the name of the Lord.

1750. Pray that the Holy Spirit will break the tendency to be blindly aggressive.

1751. Humble yourself before the Lord and be free from the tendency to be confrontational.

1752. Break yourself from the bondage of doubt and unbelief in the name of Jesus.

1753. Repent before the Lord of every tendency of self-importance.

1754. Cover yourself with the blood of Jesus against every seductive spirit.

1755. Break yourself from every neurotic tendencies

in the name of the Lord.

1756. Break yourself from the bondage of jealousy in the name of the Lord.

1757. Pray that you will be free from the tendency to intimidate the weak.

1758. Break the hold of the spirit that is unhappy and morose in your life.

1759. Pray for the touch of the Holy Spirit to free you from been miserly in the name of Jesus.

1760. Break the negative spirit of the feeling of worthlessness from holding your life.

1761. Break yourself free from a worrisome spirit and tendency in Jesus name.

1762. Ask the Lord to set you free from the tendencies of been a *"user"*.

1763. Receive freedom from every tendency of been unstable in the name of the Lord.

1764. Break free from the bondage of been talkative in Jesus name.

1765. Thank the Lord in advance for setting you free from the bondage of uncontrollable jealousy.

1766. Thank the Lord by faith that He has set you free from the bondage of insecurity.

1767. Repent and ask for the help of the Holy Spirit to overcome promiscuity in the name of the Lord.

1768. Receive freedom to overcome every trace of immaturity in all areas of life.

1769. Plead the blood of Jesus against the tendency to be paranoid.

1770. Confess that you shall not be enslaved by anything in Jesus name.
1771. Thank the Lord for setting you free from the spirit and tendency of a loser.
1772. Repent of the attitude and tendencies to be manipulative.
1773. Ask the Lord to break you free from the attitudes of a *"loner"*.
1774. Surrender to the Holy Spirit and ask Him to set you free from passive-aggression.
1775. Proclaim your freedom from the tendency of paranoia in the name of the Lord.
1776. Repent and ask the Holy Spirit to cleanse your heart from every kind of lewdness.
1777. Ask the Holy Spirit to break the power of the hold of scepticism on your heart.
1778. Declare yourself free and not a slave to any form of bondage in Jesus name.

CONFESSION

I give God praise for freedom, which He has given me in the Holy Spirit. I thank the Lord for He had made me totally victorious over every binding spirit. In the name of the Lord Jesus, I am free from the bondage of depression, I am free from the tendency of a spirit of desperation and my heart is free from a fault-finding spirit. I am not defeated.

I am filled with the spirit of boldness. I overcome every tendency that is contrary to the presence of the Holy Spirit. I am a child of God and He gives me victory over every doubtful spirit, unhealthy competition and the tendency to be blindly aggressive.

By faith, I confess that the blood of Jesus works in my life against every seductive spirit and sets me totally free form every tendency of the enemy.

I confess that I am free from the spirit of unhappiness and depression. The spirit of the Lord breaks me free from the feeling of worthlessness. I am totally free from every tendency of being unstable. By faith, I confess that the Holy Spirit has given me victory in every area of my life and I am growing in the grace of Jesus Christ, overcoming daily by the spirits word.

I am not a slave to any form of bondage but totally free in Jesus Christ.

I am blessed and highly favoured.

FRUITFULNESS

Genesis 17:6	Genesis 17:20	Genesis 28:3
Genesis 41:52	Genesis 43:11	Genesis 49:22
Exodus 1:7	Psalm 1:3	Psalm 89:20-21
Psalm 92:14	Psalm 107:34	Psalm 107:37
Psalm 127:3	Psalm 128:3	Psalm 132:11
Proverbs 8:19	Proverbs 11:30	Proverbs 12:14
Proverbs 13:2	Proverbs 18:20-21	Proverbs 27:18
Proverbs 31:16	Proverbs 31:31	Isaiah 29:17
Isaiah 32:15-16	Isaiah 57:19	Jeremiah 23:3
Ezekiel 17:5	Ezekiel 36:11	Habakkuk 3:17-19
Matthew 13:23	Mark 4:20	Mark 4:28
Luke 8:15	Acts 14:17	Romans 7:4
Colossians 1:6		

1779. Receive the power for establishment in the area of your calling in Jesus name.

1780. Pray that fruitfulness will follow the move of God that is coming in the name of Jesus.

1781. Ask the Lord to give you a heart of meekness and humility to receive His word.

1782. Confess by faith that you shall be surrounded by the fruit of you confession.

1783. Thank the Lord for His promise to make you

fruitful in all things.

1784. Prophesy fruitfulness to every area of your ministry in the name of Jesus.

1785. Confess that you will not bring forth for trouble or gather your possession for the day of adversity.

1786. Pray that the result of your labour will be fruitfulness.

1787. Give God praise for causing you to have victory at all times.

1788. Bless the name of the Lord for His faithfulness at all times.

1789. Pray that your life will be the kind of brings forth fruit at all seasons.

1790. Thank the Lord for planting you where the water of His word flows everyday.

1791. Thank the Lord for delivering you from spiritual barrenness.

1792. Pray that you will experience fruitfulness in the area where there has been barrenness in your life.

1793. Pray that you will increase in fruit bearing everyday.

1794. Pray that your fruitfulness will extend to the generations to come.

1795. Pray for those who are trusting God for the fruit of the womb that God will give them their miracle.

1796. Ask the Lord to help you so that the fruit you bear brings glory to God.

1797. Prophecy to every thing you do that increase will follow you in the name of Jesus.

1798. Praise God for His promise to make you bring forth fruit in old age.

1799. Pray that even in your old age you will still be bearing fruit that brings glory to God.

1800. Ask the Lord to prune every area of your life which does not glorify God.

1801. Pray that the fruit of patience will be manifest in your life in the name of Jesus.

1802. Ask God for the grace to accept the chastisement of the Lord and to use it to grow.

1803. Pray that your wife will give birth to the children that will bring glory to God.

1804. Command that every of barrenness in your life will break forth with fruit bearing.

1805. Ask the Lord to help you to move from mere fruit bearing to bearing much fruit.

1806. Thank the Lord for putting His blessing on everything that is still in seed form in your life.

1807. Pray that your progenitors will bring forth fruit in the name of Jesus.

1808. Pray for a transformation in every area of challenge in your life.

1809. Pray that God will turn the place of your enslavement to the land of fruitfulness.

1810. Thank the Lord for transforming your life from one degree of fruitfulness to another.

1811. Pray that every venture you go into will bear

fruit exceedingly.

1812. Confess that you shall eat the fruit of your labour in Jesus name.

1813. Pray that you will enjoy the fruit of your serving the Lord.

1814. Ask the Lord to put His blessing on the labour of your hand in Jesus name.

1815. Pray that you will be a partaker of the initiatives you are involved in.

1816. Confess your desire and believe that it shall come to pass in the name of Jesus.

1817. Pray that you will receive the grace to wait for your breakthrough and not be in haste.

1818. In your trying times when there is no fruit following your effort, still praise the Lord.

1819. Thank the Lord for His promise of creating the fruit of your lips.

CONFESSION

I believe and confess that the Lord is good, He causes me to have victory at all times. Through Him, fruitfulness follows everything I do. I am the planting of the Lord therefore fruitfulness follows wherever I am. The grace of the Lord delivers me from spiritual barrenness, God brings fruitfulness in every area where there has been barrenness in my life in the name of Jesus. I am increasing everyday in my fruit bearing.

I boldly confess, that increase follows everything I do, I shall still bear fruit that brings glory to God in old age. I shall bear the fruit of patience in my life in the name of Jesus. By faith, I command that every barrenness in my life will break forth into fruitfulness. I shall see my children's children and blessings in all that I do. The Lord will turn the place of my enslavement to the place of fruitfulness. The Lord will transform my life from one degree of fruitfulness to a greater one.

I confess by faith, the blessings of the Lord on the labour of my hand, I declare that I am a partaker of the initiatives I am involved in and in my trying times, fruit will follow my effort and I shall have reasons to praise God at all times for I shall see the fruit of my lips created for I am blessed and highly favoured.

FUTURE

Psalm 1:6   Psalm 128:6   Isaiah 34:14
Matthew 6:30   Matthew 6:34   Roman 8:28
2 Corinthians 10:4-5   Philippians 1:6   Philippians 3:14
Hebrews 12:2   Hebrews 13:5

1820. Receive the grace to focus on the mark of
      your calling.
1821. Thank the Lord because He began a good
      work in you and will complete it.
1822. Pray that the Lord will uphold you to the end
      of your Christian race.
1823. Ask the Lord to help you not to end in the
      flesh the race you began in the spirit.
1824. Pray that you will finish the Christian race and
      service well in Jesus name.
1825. Ask the Lord to help you so that your striving
      will cause you to obtain a crown.
1826. Pray for the kind of breakthrough that will
      bless your future generation.
1827. Pray that the favour of the Lord will go with

you everywhere you are in the name of Jesus.

1828. Destroy every impending trouble even before it arises in the name of the Lord.

1829. Ask the Lord to help you forget past achievements and focus on the challenges ahead.

1830. Reject and refuse every programme, vision and task that is not God's calling for your life.

1831. As was spoken into the life of Rebecca, confess that one day your children will possess the gates of their enemies.

1832. Thank the Lord in advance for helping you finish your race with joy.

1833. Give God the glory for leading you this far in your Christian walk.

1834. Thank Him for the promise not to withhold good things from those who trust Him.

1835. Thank the Lord also because He has promised not to leave or forsake you.

1836. Further more thank Him for promising to give you a future and a hope.

1837. Commit your marriage to the Lord and pray that it will get better daily in the name of the Lord.

1838. Pray that the subsequent years of your marriage will bring blessing and glory to God.

1839. Possess the future for your children by prophesying blessing into their future.

1840. Thank the Lord because everything you experience will work together for your good.

1841. Take authority over those negatives in your life that want to cloud your future.

1842. Commit your work into God's hand and pray that the years to come will carry His manifest blessing.

1843. Pray for the opening of your eyes so that you will spend your future in the job of your destiny.

1844. Pronounce the blessing of the Lord on the future of everything that has to do with your life.

1845. Confess daily that the Lord will be your shepherd and you will not miss it in life.

1846. Thank the Lord in advance for the hedge He has already built into your future.

1847. Pray for all the members of your family that their future will be in agreement with God's programme for their lives.

1848. Build a hedge of protection around your family in the name of Jesus.

1849. Refuse every excess weight or distraction which the enemy may want to use against your future.

1850. Ask the Holy Spirit to sever you from all time wasters in the name Jesus.

1851. Reject and refuse every negative confession made into your life.

1852. Pray that the vision you have started will be accomplished in the name of the Lord.

1853. Sever yourself from those who will influence

THE POWER OF POSITIVE PRAYER

your future in a negative way.

1854. Receive the anointing to follow the programme of God for your future with strong commitment.

1855. Pray for the grace to overlook, the jeers, criticisms and negatives that may come from jealous people.

1856. Ask the Lord to fill you with His peace as you face the future.

1857. Take authority over every fear of the future and receive deliverance in the name of Jesus.

1858. By faith confess that you will enter and possess your future in Christ.

1859. Pray for the wisdom to plan and implement God's programme for your future.

1860. Thank the Lord because He will make success to attend everything you do.

1861. Thank God because He will make ways for you in places higher than you can imagine.

1862. Pray for your future relationship with the Holy Spirit that it will be better everyday.

CONFESSION

I bless the Name of the Lord for His daily leading. I thank Him for not withholding any good thing from me, because I trust Him.

I boldly confess that all things will work together for my good, because I love the Lord. The future of my marriage is secure in the Lord. The future of my children is secure in the Lord. My future will portray God's manifest blessing.

I boldly confess that the Lord is my Shepherd, therefore, I shall not miss my purpose, for the Lord has built His hedge around me to give me protection and guarantees my future. Everything I lay my hand on shall be accomplished, for the Lord makes success to attend all that I do.

I am blessed and highly favoured.

GLORY

Exodus 16:7
Exodus 33:18
Deuteronomy 33:17
Psalm 8:1
Psalm 24:7-10
Psalm 111:3
Daniel 2:37
Daniel 7:14
1 Peter 1:8

Exodus 16:10
Exodus 40:34
1 Kings 8:11
Psalm 8:5
Psalm 45:3
Psalm 148:13
Daniel 4:36
2 Corinthians 4:17

Exodus 24:16
Deuteronomy 5:24
1 Chronicles 16:27-28
Psalm 15:5
Psalm 104:31
Isaiah 60:13
Daniel 5:18
1 Thessalonians 2:12

1863. Ask the Lord for the boldness to stand against whatever dishonours God's name.

1864. Pray that your motivation in serving the Lord will always be the manifestation of His glory.

1865. Ask the Lord to help you to stand against the reward which comes from destroying others.

1866. Release the fire of God on all the pile of junk that is hindering the move of God.

1867. Pray that these shall be the days of the manifestation of God's glory in your life.

1868. Thank the Lord for His glorious presence in your life at all times.

1869. Thank the Lord because the whole earth shall be filled with the knowledge of His glory.

1870. Thank the Lord for the privilege of being part of those who will manifest His glory in the last days.

1871. Pray for the church you are in, that the glory of the Lord will be released there.

1872. Pray that the Lord will be enthroned in all of the affairs of your church.

1873. Pray that the glory of the Lord will invade things that are formless and empty and turn it to pleasantness.

1874. Pray for the transformation of the things that are not bringing glory to God in your life.

1875. Ask the Lord for the grace to be yielded to Him so that you will be conformed to His image.

1876. Pray for a greater release of the shekinah glory of God than has ever been in your life.

1877. Ask the Lord to reign supreme in every aspect of your life.

1878. Pray for the fullness of time when the clouds of God's glory will be released in your life.

1879. Thank the Lord for healing the sick and setting people free as the glory increases in your church.

1880. .Thank God for the move of the spirit in your life that will make it the days of heaven on earth.

1881. Thank the Lord for the joy and peace that will follow the incoming of His glory.

1882. Pray that as you engage more in praising the Lord, glory will be produced in your church.

1883. Pray that the glory of the Lord will cause the miraculous to take place in your life.

1884. Pray that the release of the glory will also reveal the presence of the Lord in your church.

1885. Like the river in Ezekiel 47, pray that the glory of the Lord will flow out of your church and bring healing to the nations.

1886. Ask for the grace not to seek after blessing, but the release of God's glory.

1887. Begin to release the glory of God on every battle you are facing right now.

1888. Commit your worship life into God's hand that it will be the kind that creates glory.

1889. Angels only operate in the atmosphere of glory, begin to worship and create glory around you.

1890. .Pray for the manifestation fullness of Christ in the local churches in your area.

1891. Ask the Lord to structure your Christian life after His likeness and image.

1892. Ask the Lord to pour upon your life, an anointing that lingers long and brings continuous victory.

1893. Ask the Lord to clothe you with His garment of glory, salvation and righteousness.

1894. Pray for the manifestation of the splendour of God in your life.

1895. Thank the Lord for creating you to pleasure Him with praise.

1896. Ask the Lord to deliver you from all the Milchas hindering you from worship.

1897. Pray that the glory of the Lord will so fill your church, that there will be no place for sin to hide.

1898. Thank the Lord for sparking the fire of revival in your heart.

1899. Ask for the grace to wait on Him until the glory falls on that which you do.

1900. Ask the Lord to baptise you with the joy that is unspeakable and full of His glory.

CONFESSION

I believe and confess that the Lord is good. His glorious presence is manifest in my life.

I boldly confess that the earth is filled with His glory. I thank the Lord for the privilege of manifesting His glory on earth. Jesus reigns in my life and in everything I do. My ministry will bring glory, for through me He shall heal the sick, destroy bondages and set captives free. His glory fills our church.

The glory of the Lord shall be manifest in our church, in our city, and in our days.

We are blessed and highly favoured.

GROWTH

Genesis 21:8 Genesis 47:27 Deuteronomy 32:11
Psalm 92:12 Isaiah 11:1 Jeremiah 12:2
Ezekiel 47:12 Hosea 14:5 Hosea 14:7
Zechariah 6:12 Malachi 4:2 Mark 4:27
Mark 4:32 Acts 12:24 Acts 19:20
Ephesians 2:21 Ephesians 4:15 2 Thessalonians 1:3
1 Peter 2:2 2 Peter 3:18

1901. Receive the heart that is teachable and leads to honour in the name of Jesus.

1902. Pray that no matter what you go through you will be a testimony of God's good works.

1903. Give God the praise for His grace that is sufficient for all situations.

1904. Give God glory for helping you to grow from grace to grace.

1905. Pray that the word of God will find a good ground in your heart and it will bring forth fruit.

1906. Pray that you will grow in your relationship with the Lord.

1907. Pray that the seed of the word will fall on good soil in your heart in the name of the Lord.

1908. Pray that every weed of distraction that will hinder your growth will die in the name of the Lord.

1909. Pray that every relationship that will not help your growth will come to an end.

1910. Ask for the grace to ensure that your walk and association will glorify God.

1911. Pray for a deeper hunger for the word of God than you have ever known.

1912. Ask for the grace to overcome every unclean thought that sets you back in the name of the Lord.

1913. Pray that you will bear fruit in every area of your life in the name of Jesus.

1914. Ask the Lord to help you so that your life will bring glory to His name.

1915. Pray that there will constantly be manifestations of growth in your life.

1916. Thank the Lord because success will attend everything you do.

1917. Pray that everything you start will reach completion in the name of the Lord.

1918. Pray that what you began well will also end well.

1919. Give God the praise because He will help you to finish the Christian race well in the name of Jesus.

1920. Ask God for the grace to put away every immature behaviour.

1921. Pray that the Holy Spirit will help you to grow to know Him more in the name of Jesus.

1922. Ask the Lord to open your eyes to the deeper things of His.

1923. Pray that you will increase in the knowledge of the Lord.

1924. Pray that you will rise like an eagle over every situation of life.

1925. Receive by faith the leading of the Lord and thank Him because you will make it.

1926. Receive the grace of God to rise above every situation of life in the name of Jesus.

1927. Ask the Lord to help you draw wisdom from every situation you may face in the name of the Lord.

1928. Confess by faith that whatever you may be facing will turn around for your favour.

1929. Pray that you will experience an all-round growth in your Christian life.

1930. Ask the Lord to help you to be a channel of blessing to other growing Christians in the name of Jesus.

1931. Ask the Lord to help you to come to a rich understanding of the person and working of God.

1932. Receive freedom to overcome every trace of immaturity in all areas of life.

1933. Pray that you will grow in the grace to accept

the chastisement of the Lord.

1934. Pray for a heart that is tender and pliable to receive correction.

1935. Thank the Lord for His marvellous grace that is increasing unto you daily.

1936. Pray for the ability to walk in humility without feeling inferior.

1937. Ask the Lord to give you a servant's heart.

1938. Pray for the fulfilment that comes from serving other people.

1939. Ask the Lord to use your life to positively touch your generation.

1940. Pray for the spirit of God to open your eyes to the things that are childish in your life.

1941. Ask the Lord to help you move on from childish things to depth of the spirit.

1942. Pray for maturity of understanding regarding the things of the spirit.

1943. Pray that your conduct will be that which brings good testimony to the body of Christ.

1944. Ask for the grace to be rooted and grounded in Christ.

1945. Pray that you will abound in the faith and be rooted in the love of God.

1946. Thank the Lord for watching over you as you grow before Him as a tender shoot.

1947. Prophecy into all that you do that it shall grow exceedingly.

1948. Prophecy to your future that your growth shall be great, like a cedar in Lebanon.

1949. Pray that you will grow to be the temple of the Lord which He delights in.
1950. Confess by faith everything you do will grow.
1951. Thank the Lord because success will attend whatever you lay your hands on.
1952. Pray for the grace to make progress and grow like calves before the Lord.
1953. Thank the Lord for an ever-increasing faith that is operating in you.
1954. Pray for the heart that always desires the sincere word that leads to growth.
1955. Pray that you will grow in grace and in the knowledge of the Lord.
1956. Pray that you will experience an all round growth in the Lord.
1957. Prophecy to things that are still in seed form in your life that they will grow
1958. Thank the Lord because His hand of might will uphold you until you see Jesus.
1959. Spend quality time to pray for the church you belong to, that it will grow in all aspect.
1960. Thank the Lord for helping you to finish the projects you started.

CONFESSION

I believe and confess that the Lord is good. Every good word of the Lord in my life shall bring forth fruit.

I boldly declare that I have received grace to grow in my relationship with Him. The seed of God's word will fall on good soil in my life.

By faith I confess that I have received grace to walk with God and to understand His Word. His Word bears fruit in my life, for the success of the Lord attends all I do.

I boldly declare that I receive grace to put away immature behaviour and to grow more in the Lord. My eyes are open to the deeper things of God. I am increasing in the knowledge of the Lord. I soar above all situations like an eagle. I am experiencing an all round growth.

I am blessed and highly favoured.

GUIDANCE

Exodus 15:13   2 Chronicles 32:22   Psalm 25:9
Psalm 31:3   Psalm 32:8   Psalm 48:14
Psalm 73:24   Psalm 78:52   Psalm 78:72
Psalm 112:5   Proverbs 3:19   Proverbs 4:23
Proverbs 6:6-8   Isaiah 45:1-2   Isaiah 58:11
Micah 7:5   Matthew 3:16   John 16:13
Act 8:31   Romans 2:19

1961. Ask the Lord to use divine understanding to preserve you from falling into error.

1962. Pray that the favour of the Lord will go with you everywhere you are in the name of Jesus.

1963. Give thanks to God with a grateful heart for leading you daily.

1964. Thank God for the Holy Spirit who is to guide you through the darkness of this world.

1965. Yield yourself to the Lord and ask Him to guide you in your decisions.

1966. Pray that your inner ears will be tuned to hear the leading of the Lord in the midst of several voices.

1967. Commit yourself to the Lord by vowing not to

forsake Him, the guide of your youth.

1968. Ask the Lord to help you so that your trust will not be in an earthly guide.

1969. Pray that you will be led of the Lord and not take any step without Him, your guide.

1970. Ask the Lord to help you so that you are not led astray by earthly guides.

1971. At all times set the Lord as your ultimate standard and repent of your replacing Him with humans.

1972. Ask the Lord to use you to lead those who are lost to find the light.

1973. Receive the grace to be led of the Lord and not to follow the wrong crowd.

1974. Ask the Lord to expose and expunge every misleading counsellors from your life.

1975. Ask the Lord to expose every misleading counsel you may have been given in the name of Jesus.

1976. Pray that the word of God will lead and guide your life at all times.

1977. Receive the teaching and guidance of the Lord for every situation of your life.

1978. Receive God's counsel and leading for the paths you have not followed before.

1979. Thank the Lord for His promise to lead you in a straight way so that you do not stumble.

1980. Pray that as you seek the face of God you will always find clear direction.

1981. Thank the Lord for His leading you out of

great and terrible dangers in Jesus name.

1982. Thank God for directing your steps at those times when your path was full of serpents.

1983. Thank the Lord for plundering the path of evil counsellors and defeating the plan of evil judges.

1984. Thank the Lord for leading you through the Red Sea of impossible situation.

1985. Ask the Lord to direct your paths to the place of living waters in the name of Jesus.

1986. Confess that even in the deep you shall not stumble because the Lord will lead you.

1987. Confess that you are His sheep and He will lead you so that you do not miss it in life.

1988. Receive boldness not to be afraid of he who makes himself your enemy in the name of Jesus.

1989. Pray that your step will always be ordered of the Lord and you will not miss your way.

1990. Receive God's guidance in your going out and coming in, in the name of Jesus.

1991. Thank the Lord for putting every Pharaoh that wants to hold you to shame in the name of Jesus.

1992. Ask the Lord to open your eyes so that you are not led away with the workers of iniquity.

1993. Ask the Lord to uphold you in the right way so that you do not go astray or miss God's will.

1994. Thank the Lord for His goodness which has

led to your repentance and salvation in the
name of Jesus.

1995. Thank the Lord for leading you in the paths
that lead to comfort and restoration.

1996. Pray that the word of God will speak to you
and direct your path so that you will not fail or
falter.

1997. Pray that the mighty hand of God will lead
you and you will not roam around.

1998. Pray that the Lord will lead you so you do not
bring shame to His name.

1999. Thank the Lord for leading you to live above
every circumstance that is troubling you.

2000. Thank the Lord for showing you the way to go
and prospering your way.

2001. Give God praise because both day and night
the Lord will lead you and you will not fail.

2002. Give God praise for the peace in your
habitation in the name of Jesus.

2003. Rejoice in the Lord because His leading shall
be all the days of your life and you will not
fail.

2004. Humble your heart before the Lord and ask
Him to show you His way.

2005. Pray that the eye of the Lord will go with you,
guiding you in major and minor decisions.

2006. Pray for the leading of God in your career, so
that it will be carried out with discretion.

2007. Confess to the Lord how that you are lost
without His leading, and pray for His

direction.

2008. Confess, by faith that you will not fall by the way because the Lord will lead you to the end.

2009. Command a defeat for the host of the enemy and ask for the leading of God in the midst of your battle.

2010. Pray that as a believer you will not do your own thing, and bring shame to the name of the Lord.

2011. Confess that the Lord will be your leader, in times of hardship.

2012. Pray that your steps will be ordered of the Lord to the place of fruitfulness.

2013. Receive the guidance of the Holy Spirit for the understanding of His word in the name Jesus.

2014. Ask the Lord to protect you from the doctrinal errors flying around and lead you into all truth.

2015. Confess by faith that only the counsel of the Lord will stand.

2016. Receive the anointing of the Holy Spirit for the every endeavour you will embark on.

2017. Praise the name of the Lord because He will lead you to the end of your race.

2018. Confess by faith that whatever you began will be completed.

2019. Pray that the Lord will guide your life with His hand of justice and teach you His way.

2020. Pray that the eyes of the Lord will guide you so that you do not miss the purpose of God.

2021. Rejoice in the divine assurance that He is there for you when you do not know the way.

2022. Thank the Lord for holding your hand and griping your feet so it does not slip.

2023. Commit all the challenges of your life to the Lord and pray for His guidance.

2024. Pray for the divine direction of God so that it is His counsel that stands in your life.

2025. Pray that you will hear the voice of God to give you clear direction in the name of Jesus.

2026. Pray that you will not follow the opinion of the crowd but that of God.

2027. Pray that you will be led of the Lord to the place of your breakthrough in the name of the Lord.

CONFESSION

I believe and confess that the Lord is good. I rejoice before Him with gratefulness for His daily leading. The Spirit of the Lord is my guide through the darkness of this world. He orders my steps so that I do not fear.

I boldly confess that my confidence is in the Lord and not an earthly guide. He leads me and shows me the way. The hand of the Lord shall lead me in my career. My steps are ordered to the place of fruitfulness. I receive the anointing of the Holy

Spirit for every endeavour I embark on. He will lead me to accomplish what I began.

I am blessed and highly favoured.

HEALING

2 Kings 2:21 | 2 Kings 20:5 | 2 Kings 20: 8
2 Chronicles 7:14 | 2 Chronicles 30:20 | Psalm 6:2
Psalm 30:2 | Psalm 41:4 | Psalm 43:5
Psalm 103:3 | Psalm 107:20 | Psalm 147:3
Proverbs 4:22 | Proverbs 12:18 | Proverbs 13:17
Proverbs 16:24 | Ecclesiastes 3:3 | Isaiah 19:22
Isaiah 30:26 | Isaiah 57:18-19 | Isaiah 58:8
Jeremiah 3:22 | Jeremiah 17:14 | Jeremiah 30:17
Jeremiah 33:6 | Ezekiel 47:8 | Hosea 5:13
Hosea 6:1 | Hosea 11:3 | Hosea 14:4
Malachi 4:2 | Matthew 4:23 | Luke 7:3
Luke 9:11 | Acts 4:30 |

2028. Receive the bowel of mercy to touch hurting people with the love of God.

2029. Bind every sickness or disease that the enemy wants to use to stop your destiny.

2030. Break the power of the sickness that will try to hinder you from achieving your vision.

2031. Give God the praise for the opportunity to be alive and healthy today.

2032. Pray that you will be used of the Lord to heal the wounded and broken around you.

2033. Plead the blood of Jesus against every form of torment, whether physical or spiritual.

2034. Take authority over every binding disease like arthritis and command that they break their hold.

2035. Cancel the curse that may have caused spiritual barrenness in the name of the Lord.

2036. Cancel every bondage of genetic diseases in your family to ten generations.

2037. Break the hold of every evil pronouncement made into your life in the past in Jesus name.

2038. Pray that the anointing of God will flow from your life to bring healing, deliverance and hope.

2039. Thank the Lord for healing the sick and setting people free as the glory increases in your church.

2040. Release yourself by faith from every disease that may have come on you through unforgiveness.

2041. Thank God because out of your barrenness shall come forth that which glorifies God.

2042. Confess and renounce all the sins or mistakes that may have caused your barrenness.

2043. Take the time to give God the praise for His faithfulness in keeping His word.

2044. Bless His name because He will never keep any good thing from those who love Him.

2045. Take the time to give Him praise for the miracle of His healing in your life in the past.

2046. Lift His name up in praise, because He said if He is lifted up, He will draw men to Himself.

2047. Thank Him and as you do so, confess the fact that you will be healed as the brass serpent brought healing in the wilderness.

2048. Pray for the members of your household to receive the healing of the Lord.

2049. Take authority over every affliction and destroy its impact on your body in the name of Jesus.

2050. Thank the Lord for His covenant name of Jehovah Rapha.

2051. As you lay your hand on the area of your affliction, remind the Lord of His covenant to heal.

2052. Ask the Lord to remember the tears of your affliction as you call Him for prayer.

2053. Pray that the miracle of your healing will be a sign and wonder to the unsaved.

2054. Commit your business and work to the Lord and ask Him to heal the ailing area.

2055. Pray for the people who worship in your congregation and are been afflicted by the enemy, that they will be healed of the Lord.

2056. Command every disease in the bones to die in the name of Jesus.

2057. Receive inner healing for the ailments you cannot see in Jesus name.

2058. Take the time to remember and thank God for you were healed and set free from your distress.

2059. If you remember any connection between sin and the sickness, ask the Lord to forgive and heal you.

2060. Stand on His word that says He heals all diseases and confess your healing of all the diseases in your body.

2061. Take authority over every disease of the heart and receive your healing in the name of the Lord.

2062. Speak the word of God to every virus and command the viruses to die.

2063. Thank the Lord by faith and confess that the time to be healed of every diseased has come.

2064. Pray that any affliction that has come through disobedience will be healed by Him.

2065. Take authority over every trace of stroke and blood problem and receive your healing.

2066. Reject every lie of the devil that makes you think sickness glorifies God.

2067. Rejoice in the Lord because He is pleased with your ways and He will heal.

2068. The Lord says He will create the fruit of your lips, so confess your healing in Jesus name.

2069. Take a step of faith and declare your healing before the physical manifestation.

2070. Receive healing for the areas of your life that are afflicted because of your backsliding.

2071. Hand over the ailment which experts said cannot be healed and receive your healing.

2072. Take the time to acknowledge and testify the healing from the Lord.

2073. Thank the Lord for loving you so much, to be healed by the stripes of His been flogged.

2074. Ask the Lord to heal your backsliding and other areas of your Christian life that is unhealthy.

2075. Pray that every source of your blessing which may have been polluted will be healed and cleansed.

2076. Pray for your minister that God will use him to bring healing and deliverance to the people.

2077. Pray for an outbreak of healing revival in the land in the name of the Lord.

2078. Receive the anointing to bring healing to the masses of the people.

2079. Thank the Lord because His healing will flow as you praise His name.

2080. Receive the anointing to move in the power gifts of healing in the name of Jesus.

2081. Confess by faith that your healing will spring forth in the name of the Lord.

2082. Give God praise and confess that you are coming out of the bed of illness.

2083. Thank the Lord because you shall still know His power in old age.

2084. Thank the Lord because His healing will bring joy to your life.

2085. Speak the word of God to the problem area of your life and receive His healing.

2086. With your mouth, pronounce healing, deliverance, and salvation.
2087. Ask the Lord to send those who will always speak the word of life into your situation.
2088. Pray that the word of the Lord will bring healing to the innermost parts of your life.

CONFESSION

I believe and confess that the Lord is good. He is faithful at all times to keep His Word. God will not withhold good things from those who love Him. I give praise to the Lord for His work of healing in my life.

I take authority over every affliction and destroy the impact of sickness. I command diseases in the bone to die. I curse every impurity of the blood. I take authority over every disease of the heart and receive healing, in the Name of Jesus. Cancer and other destructive diseases have no power over me, for the Lord God is my Jehovah Rapha. He remembers my tears of affliction and takes away tears from members of my household.

I believe and confess that I have inner healing for ailments I cannot see. Every satanic virus is cursed to the root. Affliction is not my portion. I reject every problem of blood disease and receive healing for every area of my life.

I boldly confess that I am anointed to bring healing to the masses of the people. The Lord shall deliver those in bondage through me. The ministry of healing shall flow forth through me, in the Name of Jesus.

For I am blessed and highly favoured.

HONOUR

Exodus 14:18   Exodus 20:12   Leviticus 19:15
Leviticus 19:32   Job 22:8   Proverbs 3:9
Proverbs 3:16   Proverbs 8:18   Proverbs 13:18
Proverbs 18:12   Proverbs 21:21   Proverbs 22:4
Proverbs 25:2   Proverbs 27:18   Proverbs 29:23
Jeremiah 33:9   Isaiah 29:23   Daniel 4:34
Mark 6:4   1 Peter 2:9

2089. Thank God for counting you worthy to be among His chosen generation.

2090. Pray that at all times you will learn to hallow and honour the name of the Lord.

2091. Give God praise for the work of transformation He is doing in your life.

2092. Thank Him for teaching your heart to walk after His counsel on a day by day basis.

2093. Pray that at all times you will be clothed with the honour and glory of God.

2094. Pray that as a gracious woman retains honour, you will too.

2095. Receive the grace to walk and bring glory and

honour to the name of God.

2096. Pray that the Lord will make you a source of honour and glory to the nations of the earth.

2097. Receive the grace to honour your parents in the name of Jesus.

2098. Ask the Lord to open your eyes to the various ways you can honour those who you look up to as parents.

2099. Ask the Lord to help you walk in humility as He begins to give and your work prominence.

2100. Receive honour, riches and favour from the Lord as a blessing reserved for the righteous.

2101. Receive the grace to overcome the foolish pride that hinders blessing and honour.

2102. Pray for the wisdom to honour those who have been a blessing to you.

2103. Pray that you will not honour the Lord by lips only but with all you are and have.

2104. Ask the Holy Spirit to open your eyes to the God's honour.

2105. Receive the heart that is teachable and leads to honour in the name of Jesus.

2106. Make commit to always honour the prophets of God and receive their reward in Jesus name.

2107. Take the time to exalt the Lord for His wondrous work in your life.

2108. Make a quality decision to give all the glory that belongs to God to Him alone.

2109. As the scripture states, pray that you will

approach marriage as a thing of honour.

2110. Pray that the name of the Lord will be praised and honoured over the defeat of your enemies.

- - - - - - - - - - - - - - - - - - -

CONFESSION

- - - - - - - - - - - - - - - - - - -

I believe and confess that the Lord is good. His faithfulness is forever.

I confess that I am clothed with honour and glory and called to bring honour to the name of the Lord.

I boldly confess that the riches of God and the favour of the Lord is reserved for the righteous and flowing to me. Everything I am and everything I have honours the Lord. My heart is teachable and ready to receive His honour.

I am blessed and highly favoured.

HUNGER FOR RIGHTEOUSNESS

Psalm 1:1-3   Psalm 15:1-5   Proverbs 12:15
Isaiah 29:19   Matthew 5:6   Matthew 6:20
Matthew 6:33   Matthew 13:44-46   Luke 9:23
Romans 12:1   Romans 14:19   2 Corinthians 11:15
Philippians 3:9   Philippians 4:8   1 Peter 3:14
James 3:18

2111. Ask the Lord to give you a deeper craving for His kind of knowledge.

2112. Pray for the strength to be steadfast in the pursuit of holiness in your life.

2113. Ask the Lord to strengthen you so you do not yield yourself to unrighteousness.

2114. Ask the Lord to help you stand against the illicit reward from destroying others.

2115. Repent and ask for the help of the Holy Spirit to overcome promiscuity in the name of the Lord.

2116. Pray that the Lord will over turn the national moral decadence and spiritual depression.

2117. Pray for the prevalence of the spirit of righteousness in the land in the name of Jesus.

2118. Ask the Holy Spirit to release and increase the fruits of meekness, joy and love in you.

2119. Repent of every backbiting and evil speaking of your brothers in Christ and ask for God's forgiveness.

2120. Pray for the courage to live a godly life.

2121. Receive the grace to serve the Lord with sensitivity.

2122. Ask the Lord for the grace to keep your body from all kinds of *"lustful sins"*.

2123. Pray that you will live above every blemish the enemy wants to put on your life.

2124. Thank the Lord for His marvellous grace that leads to salvation.

2125. Praise Him for saving you from the power and penalty of sin.

2126. Pray that you will be committed to building God's kingdom.

2127. Ask the Lord for the grace to invest your time, talent and treasure in the things of the kingdom.

2128. Pray that the business of the kingdom of God will be your priority.

2129. Pray that the love of God will fill your heart.

2130. Reject and refuse every plan of the enemy to discourage you with the constant personal challenges be facing you.

2131. Thank the Lord in advance for giving you a

yielding heart.

2132. Receive the anointing to operate in holy zeal.

2133. Pray for the grace to yielded totally to the will of God.

2134. Ask the Lord for the ability to be sensitive to His spirit's leading.

2135. Receive wisdom from the Holy Spirit on how to lay all on the altar.

2136. Ask the Lord to renew your heart to appreciate the things of His kingdom.

2137. Pray for the grace to be totally committed to the cause of God's kingdom.

2138. Ask for the grace to be faithful even to the point of death and that nothing will make you backslide.

2139. Pray that you will desire righteousness in your life.

2140. Receive the grace to do only what promotes righteousness in your life in the name of Jesus.

2141. Pray that your life will reflect the grace and goodness of God.

2142. Reject and refuse any bondage of unforgiveness and lack of love in the name of Jesus.

2143. Pray that you will thirst and hunger after the purposes of God and not after carnal things.

2144. Pray that you will not glory in your own righteousness but in Christ's.

2145. Ask for the grace to endure the persecution that comes because of righteousness.

2146. Thank the Lord because He fills you with His goodness daily.

2147. Pray that the fruit of righteousness and peace will prevail in your life at all times.

2148. Thank the Lord for making you a minister of His righteousness.

2149. Reject any association or fellowship that will lead you into bondage in the name of the Lord.

2150. Pray for the ability to recognise the convicting voice of the Holy Spirit.

2151. Pray for His righteousness at all times in the name of the Lord.

CONFESSION

I believe and confess that the grace of God is sufficient for me. I have been delivered from the power and penalty of sin.

I boldly declare that everything I am and have is for the kingdom of God. My heart is yielded to do the will of God. His love fills my heart. I am anointed to operate in holy zeal.

I boldly declare that the grace of God will help me to be faithful to the end, to walk in righteousness in my life.

I receive boldness to break free from bondages,

to endure persecution. I boldly declare that the voice of the Holy Spirit will lead me and my hunger after His purpose shall increase.

I am blessed and highly favoured.

WHO I AM IN CHRIST

I am a new creature, born of God, into God's family. I am always abounding, because I have all sufficiency in all things, and abound unto every good work. I am a person who lets the peace of God rule in my heart and mind. Therefore, I am carefree about anything. Anxiety and worry do not dominate me. I choose to walk and dwell in the love of God, because I am born of God, filled with the love of God. I am a branch of the true vine. I am a member of the body of Christ.

I am rooted and grounded in the love of God, with my light shining bright. For the Lord Jesus calls me the light of the world, a city that cannot be hidden. I am an imitator of Jesus Christ, set free from the law of sin and death. I am blessed at all times, and I continually praise the Lord, because He has filled my mouth with thanksgiving.

I am accepted by the beloved, free from condemnation, delivered from the evils of this present world. I am born of God, therefore, I am born of love, and I walk and dwell in love. I am an overcomer, through the blood of the Lamb and the word of my testimony.

Daily, I overcome the devil and therefore, refuse to be moved by what I see. I am a labourer with the Lord. I am the righteousness of God in Christ Jesus, therefore, I am complete in Him. I have been transformed by the renewing of my mind, and so I bring every thought into captivity. I cast down all imaginations, and everything that exalts itself against the knowledge of Christ. I have the capacity to bring my body into subjection.

By faith I walk with God and not by sight. I call those things that are not as though they were. I call into existence things by faith. I am established in the will of God, profiting from my confession. Through Christ, I am more than a conqueror. I choose to be above only and not beneath. I am delivered from the power of darkness, translated into the kingdom of Jesus Christ. I am His sheep; the Lord is my shepherd. He leads me and guides me in the pathway of life. I am led of the Spirit of God, so I shall not miss my way. His Word calls me son. That's who I am.

I am protected wherever I go. I get all my needs met through Jesus Christ. I cast all my cares upon the Lord, choosing to be strong in the Lord and in the power of His might.

Jesus is mine and I am His. I delight myself in the Lord Jesus Christ. I acknowledge Him as the author of all things. I am a heir of God and a joint heir with Jesus Christ. I can do all things through Christ Who strengthens me. I choose to sit in the heavenly places in Christ Jesus, declaring that I am a heir to the blessing of Abraham. I choose to observe and to do the Lord's commandment.

I am blessed in my going out, and coming in. For I have inherited eternal life. I am blessed with all spiritual blessings, speaking the truth with love, growing up into Jesus Christ in all things. For I am crucified with Christ. I am dead with Christ. I am buried with Christ, and I have risen with Him. I am blood washed, cleansed, sanctified child of God. My sins are forgiven.

I am saved by grace. I am born again. I am justified fully through Calvary's love. I have been co-opted into the family of God. So I am a new creature. I am God's workmanship, a partaker of God's divine nature, pure, holy, sanctified. I am in His hand, therefore, I shall not be afraid of what man can do to me.

His Word says I am redeemed from the curse of the law, for Christ has been made a curse for me. I am healed by His stripes. No disease or sickness, virus; be it genetic or environmental, reigns over my body. My body belongs to God. I am prosperous, reigning in life through Jesus Christ, receiving daily the power to get wealth. I am above principalities and powers, and they are under my feet. Because of Jesus, I exercise authority over the enemy. I am victorious, more than a conqueror, winning every day. I am established on earth to reign with Jesus Christ.